THE LORD FROM HEAVEN

Sir Robert Anderson

The Lord from Heaven by Sir Robert Anderson. © 1978 by Kregel Publications, a division of Kregel, Inc., P.O. Box 2607, Grand Rapids, MI 49501. All rights reserved.

Library of Congress Cataloging-in-Publication Data
Anderson, Robert, Sir, 1841–1918.
    The Lord from Heaven.

    (Sir Robert Anderson library)
    1. Jesus Christ—Person and offices. I. Title. II. Series: Anderson, Robert, Sir. 1841–1918. Sir Robert Anderson Library.

| BT201.A54 | 1978 | 232 | 78-9533 |
| | | | CIP |

ISBN 978-0-8254-2579-0

1 2 3 4 5 / 12 11 10 09 08

Printed in the United States of America

CONTENTS

CONTENTS

PUBLISHER'S PREFACE

Almost a century has passed since this classic work was written by Sir Robert Anderson. Yet the controversy still rages over the same subject, "Is Jesus really God?" Despite all of the evidence that He is Divine Lord, the critics still spew their venom and the skeptics still pen their doubts. The initial conditions which prompted the writing of this book still exist . . . those who believe need new assurance for their faith, and the honest seeker for truth needs answers to his questions.

All who read this book will come away with a deeper appreciation for the Lord who bought them. For to realize what the Lord Jesus gave up, when Heaven was "robbed" of His presence, will cause all of us to fall on our spiritual knees and cry out, "My Lord and my God."

We are indeed indebted to the scholarly author who has taken this unique approach to the subject of the deity of Christ. He finds gems under the strangest rocks and hunts proofs in every nook. Lo and behold, they were there all the time, but it takes the heart of a man who knows the heart of God to find them. How grateful we should be that Sir Robert Anderson was such a man, and this labor of love is now preserved for us, so we too can taste of the riches of God in realizing WHO our Saviour really is, and what He came to do.

PUBLISHER'S PREFACE

PREFACE TO SECOND EDITION

THE publication of this book has brought me many striking proofs that a book of this kind is needed. The mass of men are unreached by learned works upon this great subject, and mere popular treatises fail to convince the thoughtful. But in these pages there is nothing which any Bible student cannot follow, and yet they contain enough to satisfy all who accept the authority of Christ as a divine Teacher, or the authority of Holy Scripture as a divine revelation. And this being the scheme of the book, I have refrained from quoting the writings of theologians; and my acquaintance with ancient controversies has been used solely to enable me to shun the heresies which provoked them.

It would seem that very many who, by habitually repeating the creeds, give a conventional assent to the doctrine of the Deity of Christ, are practically agnostics in relation to it. And to me this discovery is made still more startling by the fact that their doubts seem to be confirmed by the language of the very formulas which were intended to set the question at rest for ever. For the phrase, "the persons of the Trinity." apparently conveys a meaning wholly different from that which the original words were intended to express. And to the illiterate it suggests error which leaves them an easy prey to the Unitarian propagandist.

As the Latin Dictionary tells us, the word *persona* is "from *per-sono,* to sound through"; and it means "a mask, especially that used by players, which covered the whole head, and was varied according to the different characters to be represented." And, according to the Oxford English Dictionary, our word "person" means "(1) a character sustained or assumed in a drama, or the like, or in actual life; part played; hence function, office, capacity; (2) an individual being." It will thus be seen how closely the primary and classical signification of "person" is allied to the Latin *persona,* and what slight affinity it has with the popular and ordinary meaning of the word. And yet its ordinary meaning has a definite influence upon the minds of ordinary people when they speak of "the persons of the Trinity."

The Deity is not to be likened to a triumvirate acting in unison. God is One. But He has manifested Himself as Father, Son, and Holy Spirit; and the crowning manifestation of Himself was in the Son. At the coming of Christ He was "manifested in flesh." The somewhat doubtful revised reading of I Timothy 3:16 in no way affects the force of the passage. The statement that the Man of Nazareth "was manifested in flesh" would be nothing better than a grandiloquent platitude. "He who was manifested in flesh" must refer to God. The words are the equivalent of John 1:18, which tells us that the Son has declared Him.

But, we are asked by people who own that they are in the habit of repeating the creeds, "How could the Son be God, seeing that He prayed to God, and spoke of God as a Being distinct from His own personality?" This is a real difficulty; and it is not to be met by attempting to explain "the mystery of God, even Christ," but by freely owning that the mystery is one which reason cannot solve. How strange it is that while, on "the authority of the Church," men give an unquestioning assent to the superstitions of what they deem to be "the Christian religion," we hesitate to accept the mysteries of the Christian faith upon the authority of the Word of God! And with great humility I hazard the opinion that, in their zeal for the truth, the orthodox Fathers went to unwise lengths in analyzing and defining the Deity. But be that as it may, certain it is that the formularies of those days create difficulties in many devout minds in our own times.

In presence of the mystery of God, which, we are expressly told, we cannot fathom, our part is simply to accept the "It is written." But let us see to it that what we accept is really what is written. I am here reminded of help received many years ago from having my attention called to the Greek text of John 1:1. My lesson was learned during a railway journey, and my teacher was a Roman Catholic friend, one of H.M.'s judges of the Supreme Court, who pointed out to me the significance of the presence of the Greek article in the one clause, and its absence in the other clause, of the familiar passage.

Our English idiom fails us here; but if we might use the word "Deity" as a synonym for "God," any one could appreciate the difference between the statement that the Word was with the Deity, and the further statement that the Word was Himself Deity.

Of course the Unitarian fritters away the force of this. But even in days when the language of Scripture is treated with reckless freedom, the signficance of the words which follow cannot be evaded. For we are told, "All things were made by Him"; and if the Creator of all things be not God, language has no meaning. Classic paganism, indeed, could fall back on the figment of a subordinate God—a conception which modern enlightenment rejects—and the Arian heresy would never have gained such a hold in the Patristic Church had not the minds of so many of the Fathers been corrupted by the paganism of their early training (see p. 57 *post*). Indeed, we learn from I Corinthians 8 that even the Christians who enjoyed the benefit of direct Apostolic teaching were not wholly free from pagan error in this respect.

We need to keep this in view in reading that chapter, for the sixth verse, "To us there is one God the Father," is the Unitarian's charter text. And this, we are told, is rendered the more emphatic by the sequel, "And one Lord Jesus Christ."

And the teaching here is aimed at the pagan errors which then prevailed; and, in view of the immediate context, it is an impossible suggestion that the Apostle Paul intended to teach that the Lord Jesus Christ was but a creature. For the added words, "by whom are all things," unequivocally declare the truth which is more fully revealed in Colossians 1:15-17, that the Lord Jesus is the Creator of the universe. And if this does not assert His Deity, I again repeat, words have no meaning. He "by whom are all things" must be God. Any one, therefore, who refuses the truth that the Lord Jesus is God, must acknowledge *two* Gods.

The Christian reads the passage in the light of the words, "I and My Father are One." But, we are told, these words are to be explained by His prayer to the Father on behalf of His people, "that they may be one *even as we are One*" (John 17:22). Surely we might suppose that even a child could understand the difference between perfect unity and essential oneness. When Hooker wrote, "Our God is one, or rather very *oneness*," he was not giving expression to a mere platitude, but to divine truth about the God whom we know as Father, Son, and Holy Spirit.

The prayer of the betrayal night points to the time when the unity between His people and God will be as perfect as the unity between the Father and the Son. But that is vastly different from essential oneness. Will that unity empower them, either corporately or as individuals, to create worlds, to forgive sins, or to give life to whom they will! And these supreme prerogatives of Deity pertain to the Lord Jesus Christ. There is no escape from the dilemma in which this places us. If there be not *two* Gods, we must own that the Father and Son are *One*.

But, some one demands, "How then do you explain—?" Without waiting to hear what form the inquiry assumes, we reply at once that we do not attempt to explain "the mystery of God." "No one knoweth the Son, save the Father." And the force of this is intensified by the sequel, "Neither doth any one know the Father, save the Son, and he to whomsoever the Son willeth to reveal Him." The truth of the Fatherhood is a mystery revealed in Christ: the truth of the Sonship remains an unrevealed mystery which transcends reason, but which faith accepts. In teaching our children we often find that what to us seems clear is beyond the mental grasp of childhood; and yet we fail to recognize that divine truth may be beyond the capacity of finite minds. "Canst thou by searching find out God? Canst thou find out the Almighty to perfection?" The Arian controversy assumes that we *can!*

Heresy trades upon isolated texts, and the Unitarian heresy, as we have seen, ignores even the context of the words on which it relies. Take another striking instance of this. At the grave of Lazarus "Jesus wept." And presently "He lifted up His eyes and said, Father, I thank Thee that Thou hast heard me." What proof this gives of His humanity, and that His relation to God was that of a man dependent on the divine Father! Yes, truly; but at that same time, and in that very scene, it was that He spoke the words, "I am the resurrection and the life." No Gentile, perhaps, can fully realize what those words conveyed to a devout Jew. If He who uttered them was not divine in the fullest and most absolute sense, the men who crucified Him were obeying one of the plainest commands of the divine law in putting Him to death.

In saying this we assume, of course, that the Lord actually spoke the words attributed to Him. For these pages are addressed to Christians; and if the Gospels be not the divinely accredited records of His ministry, the Christian faith must give place to agnosticism in the case of all but the superstitious.

And while utterly rejecting the *Kenosis* theory—that our Lord's words were at times the expression of divine truth, and at other times of Jewish error—we may notice that, as these particular words were in such violent opposition to all Jewish thought, they must, even on that profane hypothesis, be accepted as divine.

With some people religious doctrines seem to be kept in water-tight compartments. And thus they can hold divine truth along with human error which conflicts with it. But truth is really one, and if any part be assailed the whole is imperiled. If, for example, we let go the Deity of Christ, which is the foundation truth of Christianity, the doctrine of the Atonement is destroyed. For in the whole range of false religions there is not a more grotesquely silly superstition than that the death of a fellow-creature could expiate the sin of the world.

But in these days the need of expiation is largely ignored. And this because the ordinary conception of sin is so inadequate as to be practically false. Therefore it is that the truth of the Lord's Deity is held so lightly. For men are content with a vague belief in reconciliation brought about in some undefined way by the example of a perfect life and a self-sacrificing death. And even this is lost by those who adopt the figment that the Lord belonged to a higher type of creaturehood than humanity. Certain it is that He who died for men must Himself be man. And yet were He only man His death would avail us nothing; for, as the Bishop of Durham puts it, "A Saviour not quite God is a broken bridge at the farther end."

And we must be on our guard against another error. The popular conception of "a divine man," "a God-man," a being half human and half divine, savors of old-world paganism. The Lord Jesus Christ is "very man" and yet "very God." He is the "type" and pattern of humanity, and yet He is the Son of God in all which that title signifies. He is the only God the world shall ever know. Apart from Him "no one has ever seen God": apart from Him no one of mankind can ever see Him.

And He it is who died for us. For "He who knew no sin was made sin for us." And if it be demanded how this could be, we answer with Bishop Butler, "All conjectures about it must be, if not evidently absurd, yet at least uncertain." "And," as he adds, "no one has any reason to complain from want of further information unless he can show his claim to it." God here retreats upon His divine Sovereignty, and faith accepts the divine "It is written."

But everything depends upon the Deity of Christ; and, therefore, as Athanasius said long ago, in contending for that great truth "we are contending for our all."

R. A.

INTRODUCTION

SOME years ago the author was asked to mediate between the Committee of one of our Missionary Societies and certain of their younger agents, whose faith had been disturbed by Moslem hostility to the truth of the Sonship of Christ. Though not unversed in the literature on the subject, he could find no book that definitely met the difficulties of the missionaries, and the project of writing such a book was suggested to him. And a recent correspondence disclosed the fact that, by those who deny the Lord's Deity, that truth is supposed to depend on the special texts which teach it explicitly.

These pages accordingly seek to unfold the doctrine of the Sonship, and to call attention to some of the indirect testimony of Scripture to the Deity of Christ. The book is not controversial. It is a Bible study. And if the perusal of it proves as helpful to any, as the writing of it has been to the author, its purpose will be satisfied.

He wishes here to acknowledge help received in the preparation of it. To the Bishop of Durham he is under very special obligations for kindly and valuable criticism and counsel. And his labors were lightened by his friend, Miss A. R. Habershon, who, besides aid freely given in other ways, prepared for his use a New Testament "concordance" of the names and titles of the Lord Jesus Christ.

It may be well to mention that in these pages the references to Scripture do not specify which of our Versions is quoted, save where it is desired to call special attention to the reading adopted.

1

THE QUESTION AT ISSUE

"THE great English philosopher, John Stuart Mill, has somewhere observed that mankind cannot be too often reminded that there was once a man of the name of Socrates. That is true; but still more important is it to remind mankind again and again that a man of the name of Jesus Christ once stood in their midst."

These are the opening sentences of a well-known work from the pen of the greatest Rationalists of this century.[1] But in this twentieth century such a reminder is an anachronism. For infidelity has changed its ground, and the facts of the life and ministry of Christ no one now denies. The only question in dispute today relates to His personality. Who and what was the Great Teacher whose advent changed the history of the world?

As the result of the controversies which raged around that question in the early centuries, the creed of Christendom proclaims His Deity. But in these days the creed of Christendom has been thrown into the melting-pot. And the real aim of the Christianized Rationalist, concealed beneath a cloak of Christian terminology, is to prove that the "Jesus Christ" who once stood in our midst was but a man.

And the great problem of the ages has today assumed a new and subtle phase. For that which was formerly the issue in the Unitarian controversy is no longer in dispute. The *divinity* of Christ is now acknowledged even by the infidel. "Rest now in thy glory!" Renan exclaims in an out-

[1]Prof. Adolf Harnack's "What is Christianity?"

burst of enthusiastic homage. "Thy work is achieved, thy divinity established. . . . Between thee and God men shall distinguish no longer." Indeed it is accepted even by the base apostasy which masquerades as "the New Theology."

For, we are told, God is "immanent" in human nature, and we are all His sons. The Nazarene's title to divinity therefore is not only undisputed, but it is admittedly pre-eminent, albeit it is not exclusive. Every prince of the blood is a royal personage. But not even the Prince of Wales, unique though his position be, has either the power or the dignity of kingship. The parable needs no interpreting: the question at issue today is not the divinity of Christ, but His DEITY.

In dark days now past, when the avowal of "heretical" beliefs involved suffering and loss, men thought deeply before they strayed from the beaten tracks of "orthodoxy." They knew what it meant to "gird up the loins of their mind." But slovenly-mindedness is a marked characteristic of religious thought in this shallow and silly age of ours. The catch phrases of the fashionable pulpit or the popular press are accepted without any sort of mental struggle; and "historic beliefs" are jettisoned without the slightest exercise of heart or conscience. And yet, having regard to the transcendent importance and solemnity of the question here at issue, such levity is intolerable. For if the "historic beliefs" are true, the coming of Christ was the crisis of the world.[2]

While then, with the Rationalist, the Great Teacher was "a man of the name of Jesus Christ," the Christian maintains His Deity. This belief, moreover, is based on the writings of His first disciples; and if the beliefs of the Apostles and other writers of the New Testament on a subject of such supreme importance do not reflect the teaching of their

[2]See John 12:31.

Lord, and of the Holy Spirit who was given to guide them into all truth, faith in Christianity is mere superstition.

That the New Testament teaches the Deity of Christ is so indisputable that the infidel accepts the fact, and the task he sets himself is to disparage the testimony of the writers. In Baur's day this was achieved by maintaining that most of the sacred books were not written by the men whose names they bear, but belong to a later age. It is achieved in our day by insisting that, just because the writers were His disciples, they were not impartial witnesses, and their evidence is therefore unreliable.

Such are the ways of those who attack the Bible. "The Tübingen school"[3] implicitly allowed that if the New Testament had been written by the Lord's contemporaries, the evidence would be valid. The Schmiedel school today insist that, just because the writers were His personal disciples, they were not impartial, and their evidence should be rejected! To put it tersely, no one who believed in His claims should be allowed a hearing in support of His claims.

The conception of a tribunal which acted on this principle would be delightful in a "nonsense book" or in a farce to be acted on the stage. It is a theory of evidence unknown in any civilized community—ancient or modern. And no less absurd would it be if applied to history. Suppose, for example, a life of Queen Victoria written on the system of excluding everything derived from those who knew and honored her!

---

[3]It might be in order to say that this is a term applied to a theological movement which had its origins in the teachings of Ferdinand Christian Baur, of the University of Tübingen, in Germany. His distinctive and guiding principles were those of the Hegelian philosophy. It was his aim to reconstruct the history of early Christianity so that it would be seen to be in harmony with the laws which supposedly govern historical evolution. Accordingly he supposed a conflict between the teachings of Paul and of Peter. But after Paul's death a reconciliation was effected which resulted in the establishment of the old Catholic Church.

How, then, does the matter stand? Upon the question here at issue, the testimony of the disciples is so clear that even the infidel acknowledges that it would deserve acceptance if it were confirmed by independent evidence. But no confirmatory evidence is more convincing than that of hostile witnesses, and the fact that the Lord laid claim to Deity is incontestably established by the action of His enemies. We must remember that the Jews were not a tribe of ignorant savages, but a highly cultured and intensely religious people; and it was upon this very charge that, without a dissentient voice, His death was decreed by the Sanhedrin—their great national Council, composed of the most eminent of their religious leaders, including men of the type of Gamaliel and his great pupil, Saul of Tarsus.

That He was of the royal house of David was proved by the official genealogies. That He did great miracles was universally acknowledged, and not even His enemies denied that all His acts and, *save on one vital point,* all His words, were worthy of His Messianic claims. How, then, can the fact be accounted for that good men—men who had a zeal for God—condemned Him to death as a blasphemer? The answer is not doubtful. It was not for His good deeds that He had been threatened with stoning, but because, said they, "Thou, being a man, makest Thyself God." And upon this charge it was, I repeat, that He was arraigned. Had that charge been false, had it been due to a perversion of His words, He would, as a devout Jew, have repudiated it with indignant earnestness, whereas His acceptance of it was unequivocal.

"Not so," the Unitarian will object, "the accusation was not that He claimed to be God, but that He called Himself *the Son of God;* and the answer He gave—that He was yet to sit 'on the right hand of power'—was in keeping with all His teaching. The very assertion of His Sonship was itself an acknowledgment that He took a subordinate place, and owned the Supreme as His Father and His God."

Are we to conclude, then, that the crucifixion of Christ was due to a misunderstanding which any one of us might have put right, if only we could have gained a hearing before the Sanhedrin on that fateful day? The alternative to this absurd suggestion is that the assertion of His Sonship was essentially to Deity. And this suggests an inquiry of extreme interest and importance respecting the use and meaning of the word "son" in the New Testament.

2

MEANING OF "SON" IN SCRIPTURE

IT IS unnecessary to notice passages where the word "son" stands for remote descendant, as, for example, in the first verse of the first Gospel, or in the familiar phrase "Children of Israel,"[1] or again, when the Lord declared that in building the tombs of the prophets the Jews bore witness that they were the "sons" of those who slew them.[2] Still less need we notice the numerous occurrences of the word in its primary and common acceptation. But such is the influence of our English Bible upon our habits of thought and speech that when we are told that James and John were "sons of thunder" the phrase seems as natural as when we read that they were sons of Zebedee. Our *English* Bible, I say advisedly; for when the Revised Version first appeared, people were inclined to resent such unfamiliar phrases as "sons of the bridechamber," and "sons of disobedience." And yet the distinction between "son" and "child" is of great importance; and in ignoring it our translators have sometimes obscured, or even perverted, vital truth.

In the Sermon on the Mount, for instance, the Lord seems to say that by loving their enemies men may become children of God. But this is utterly opposed to Christian teaching. It is by birth, and only by birth, that the relationship of father and child can be created. Moreover the Lord was there addressing His disciples.[3]

[1]The word in the original is *Sons* of Israel.
[2]Matthew 23:29-31. [3]Matthew 5:44, 45.

Again, the A.V. reads, "As many as received him, to them gave he power to become the sons of God, even to them that believe on his name, which were born . . . of God."[4] But this is no less inaccurate. Thus it is indeed that we become *children* of God, and "children" is the word here used; but sonship connotes what children ought to be. "As many as are led by the Spirit of God, these are *sons* of God."[5]

To many the statement may seem startling, but its truth can be easily tested, that in the New Testament believers in Christ, as such, are never designated *sons* of God. In other words, that phrase never occurs as a mere synonym for "children of God." The words of Galatians 3:26 may seem to be an exception to this, but in fact they afford a striking illustration of it. For when the Apostle writes, "Ye are all the sons of God, through faith, in Christ Jesus," he uses the word "sons" in a peculiar sense, his purpose being to mark the difference between the position of children under age, and of those who have attained their majority. In this Christian dispensation the people of God are no longer treated as in a state of nonage, "under tutors and governors," but are now deemed to be of full age, and take rank as *sons.*[6]

In Hebrews 12:8, again, the word "sons" occurs in a sense equally foreign to our English use for it marks the distinction between the legitimate offspring and the illegitimate, to the latter of whom the status of *son* is denied.

These two passages are quite exceptional, the word "son" being employed to connote dignity or privilege, whereas it is generally used to indicate character or nature. And it is noteworthy that when the word is employed in this ethical sense, no thought of parentage is involved, unless, perhaps, remotely, and by way of a poetic figure. The Gentile Galatian

---

[4]John 1:12, 13.
[5]Romans 8:14, R.V.; *cf.* II Corinthians 6:17, 18.
[6]See Galatians 4:1-5, and Alford *in loco.*

converts, for example, could have no possible claim to be "children of Abraham," nor would the Apostle have thus described them; but, though not "sons of the stock of Abraham,"[7] he tells them that "they which are of faith, the same are *sons* of Abraham."[8] The word is here used as definitely in a figurative sense, as in the phrase "sons of thunder."

And that phrase might teach us to distinguish between the traditional "St. John" and the Apostle of that name. The one was a soft, womanly creature, whereas "the beloved disciple" was a bold and manly man who used strong, stern words. For with him those who cherish malice are murderers; and those who belittle the Lord Jesus Christ, or deny His glory, are liars and anti-Christs. And remembering that his brother, the Apostle James, was a man of the same type, we can well understand why his death was specially pleasing to the Jews when he fell as a victim of Herod's malignity.

If Joseph (or Joses) had been called "a child of consolation," we might suppose him to have been the recipient of very special comfort; but when we read that the Apostles surnamed him Barnabas, or "*son* of consolation,"[9] we conclude that he was a man of intensely sympathetic spirit.

In the same way "sons of wrath" would be Greek for the Hebrew "sons of Belial"; but when the Epistle to the Ephesians tells us that by nature we are "*children* of wrath," the words are meant to express our condition and destiny. So, again, the phrase "a child of disobedience" might perhaps imply that the individual was the progeny of a parent's sin, whereas "sons of disobedience" describes what men are essentially and as to their very nature.[10]

---

[7]Acts 13:26. The R.V. is in error here. The word is "sons."
[8]Galatians 3:7.
[9]Acts 4:36.
[10]Ephesians 2:2, 3, and 5:6 (Col. 3:6).

The fact that the Apostle exhorts the Ephesians to walk as *"children* of light," whereas *"sons* of light" is his word to the Thessalonians,[11] may seem to indicate that in this instance, at least, the words are used as synonyms. But an examination of the passages will make it clear that here, as elsewhere, the words carry their distinctive meanings. The one statement describes the normal condition and environment of the Christian the other relates to his character and nature. There is a double parallel: "Watch and be sober" answers to "Walk as children of light," but "Ye are all sons of light" answers to "Ye are light in the Lord."

This may remind us of the Lord's words in explaining the Parable of the Unjust Steward: "The sons of this world are for their own generation wiser than the sons of the light."[12] The comparison here is not between earth and heaven, but between those who belong morally to the present economy and those who are "light in the Lord." But in another passage, where the Lord speaks of "sons of this world" and "sons of the resurrection," the contrast is merely between our condition in the present economy, and what we shall be when we "attain to that world."[13] He thus uses the phrase in a double sense. In the one case, "sons of this world (or age)" includes all who belong to this economy in the sense of being *in* it, whereas in the parable it indicates those who are *of* it.

Nor will this seem strange if we keep in mind that in Scripture the word bears an Oriental and essentially figurative meaning. And this is true, even where a literal sense might seem possible, as for example, when the Apostle Peter appeals to the Jews as "sons of the prophets."[14] His audience

[11]Ephesians 5:8; I Thessalonians 5:5.
[12]Luke 16:8.
[13]Luke 20:34-36.
[14]Acts 3:25.

may, of course, have included some who were actual descendants of the prophets; but the words he added, "and *of the covenant*," make it clear that no such thought was in his mind. In addressing them as "sons of the prophets and of the covenant," he was appealing to them as heirs of the hopes and promises of which the covenant and the prophecies spoke.

So again, when the Apostle Paul denounced Elymas the sorcerer as "Thou son of the devil,"[15] his Oriental hearers would understand his words as describing the man's character and nature. And in this same sense it was that the Lord Himself branded the typical proselyte of the Pharisees as a "son of hell."[16]

---

[15]Acts 13:10.
[16]Matthew 23:15.

3

THE SON OF MAN

THIS preliminary inquiry will help us to appreciate the significance of the word "Son" in the titles of our Divine Lord. And first as to His self-chosen designation of Son of Man. Is it, as the Rationalist and the Jew would tell us, a mere Hebraism meaning no more than that He was human? The English reader misses the significance which the Greek article lends to the words in the original. But it is recognized by scholars; and those who wish to evade it maintain that the Lord spoke in Palestinian Aramaic, and in that dialect, they declare, the phrase could not have the meaning which the Christian assigns to it. But we can afford to ignore discussions of this kind. For words are like counters, in that their value is settled by those who use them; and there can be no doubt as to the significance which the Lord Himself attached to this His favorite title.

When, for example, He exclaimed, "The foxes have holes and the birds of the air have nests, but the Son of man hath not where to lay his head,"[1] it is clear that the contrast implied in His words was between the highest and the lowest. The humblest creatures had a home, but He, "the firstborn of all creation,"[2] was an outcast wanderer. This is the first occurrence of the phrase in the New Testament, and in Scripture a first occurrence is often specially significant. And certain it is that on the last occasion on which He used the title—it was when on His defense before the Sanhedrin—His purpose was, by declaring Himself to be the

[1]Matthew 8:20.
[2]Colossians 1:15, R.V.

Son of Man of Daniel's vision, to assert His claim to heavenly glory.[3]

For while the first vision of the seventh chapter of Daniel (like the vision of the second chapter) is of earthly kingdoms in relation to Israel and Israel's Messiah, the vision which follows, in which He is seen as "Son of Man" in heaven, reveals a wider sovereignty and a higher glory. In many a learned treatise the question is discussed whether this be a Messianic title at all; and in not a few this question becomes merged in an inquiry whether the Jew regarded it as such. But the Lord's words before the Sanhedrin clearly point to the conclusion suggested by His use of the title in the passage already cited, namely that it was His rejection as Messiah that led Him to declare Himself the Son of Man.[4]

And this conclusion is confirmed by the record of the martyr Stephen's vision. His murder was Jerusalem's final rejection of Messiah. For he was the messenger sent after the King to say they would not have Him to reign over them. And as his eyes were closing upon this world, they were opened to see the heavenly vision Daniel saw—"the Son of Man on the right hand of God."[5]

It was not His human birth that constituted Him the Son of Man. That birth, indeed, was the fulfilment of the promise which the name implied; but the Son of Man, He declared explicitly, "descended out of heaven."[6] And He said again, "What and if ye shall see the Son of man ascend

---

[3]Without attempting to limit the meaning of His saying, "the Son of Man which is in heaven" (John 3:13), it certainly implies "whose place is in heaven" (Alford). It is a heavenly title, therefore, and a heavenly glory.

[4]His crucifixion was the climax of a rejection that declared itself at the very beginning of His ministry. "He came unto His own, and His own received Him not."

[5]Acts 7:56. Cf. Luke 19:14.

[6]John 3:13.

up where he was before?"[7] When, therefore, He proclaims that "the Son of man came to seek and to save that which was lost,"[8] came "to give his life a ransom for many,"[9] faith responds intelligently in the words of that noblest of the Church's hymns, "When Thou tookest upon Thee to deliver man, Thou didst not abhor the Virgin's womb." For the virgin birth was but a stage in the fulfilment of His mission.

Nor was it as the Virgin's Son, but as the Son of Man, that He claimed to be "Lord even of the Sabbath," and to have "power upon earth to forgive sins." And, according to the language of our English Versions, it is as the Son of Man that the prerogative of judgment has been committed to Him. The Father, He said, "hath given him authority to execute judgment also, because he is the Son of Man."[10] But a reference to the original discloses the fact that here the form of the words suggests that His purpose is to emphasize that it is because He is MAN that He is appointed to be the judge of men.[11]

The revelation of the Son of Man will lead the spiritual Christian, who has learned to note the hidden harmony of Scripture, to recall the language of the creation story: "Let us make man in our image, after our likeness."[12] "The type," as the biologist would phrase it, is not the creature of Eden,

[7]John 6:62.
[8]Luke 19:10.
[9]Matthew 20:28.
[10]John 5:27.
[11]Eighty times the words "Son of Man" occur as uttered by the Lord; but here, and here alone, they are anarthrous (see p. 29 *ante*). Bishop Middleton maintains ("The Greek Article," p. 246) that the absence of the articles makes no difference; and he accounts for it by saying that "Now, for the first time, has Christ *asserted* His claim to the title: in all other places He has assumed it." But surely this would be a valid reason only if this were either the first time, or the last, of His using the words.
[12]Genesis 1:26.

but He after whose likeness the creature was fashioned. And this suggests the solution of a "mystery." We are but *men,* and while angels behold the face of God, no *man* hath seen Him or can see Him.[13] We are "flesh and blood," and "flesh and blood cannot inherit the kingdom of God."[14] And yet *as men* we are to dwell in heavenly glory; and that wonderful promise shall be fulfilled to us—"They shall see his face."[15]

How is this seeming paradox to be explained? "Flesh and blood" are not essential to humanity. True it is that, as "the children are partakers of flesh and blood, He also Himself likewise took part of the same."[16] He assumed "a natural body." "For there is a natural body, and there is a spiritual body." The one pertains to the "first man," who is "of the earth earthy," the other to "the second Man," who is "of heaven."[17] For the Lord from heaven is "Very Man," and it is as Man that He is now upon the throne. But the body is not the man: it is but the tent, the outward dress, as it were, which covers Him. And He is "the same yesterday, and today, and for ever";[18] the same who once trod the roads of Galilee and the streets of Jerusalem. He is enthroned as Man, but no longer now in "flesh and blood." For ere He "passed through the heavens" He changed His dress.

And we too "shall be changed." "As we have borne the image of the earthy, we shall also bear the image of the heavenly." The image, or pattern, of the earthy is the Adam of the Eden creation; that of the heavenly is the last Adam, the Lord from heaven. And He will "fashion anew the body of our humiliation, that it may be conformed to the body of

---

13I Timothy 6:16.
14I Corinthians 15:50.
15Revelation 22:4.
16Hebrews 2:14.
17I Corinthians 15:44, 47.
18Hebrews 13:8. *Cf.* 1:12.

his glory."[19] For the triumph of redemption will not be in restoring us to the place which Adam lost by sin, but in raising us to the perfectness of the new creation, of which the Lord from heaven is the head. The eyes of our faith are not fixed upon the blessedness of Eden, but upon the glory of "the Holy Mount"; for "we know that when he shall appear we shall be like him, for we shall see him as he is."[20]

We must bear in mind, then, the distinction so clearly marked in Scripture between the Lord's essential glory as the Son of Man, and what He became in virtue of His human birth. Nor is this all. We need to remember also that, because of His humiliation, He has been raised to a position and a glory beyond what is revealed in the Hebrew Scriptures, or even in the doctrinal teaching of the Gospels. "He humbled himself, becoming obedient even unto death, yea, the death of the cross. Wherefore also God highly exalted him and gave unto him the name which is above every name."[21]

In view of His prayer on the night of the betrayal, how can this be understood? "And now," He said, "O Father, glorify thou me with thine own self, with the glory which I had with thee before the world was."[22] A higher glory is inconceivable, and this glory was His by right: what meaning, then, can be given to the statement that He was raised to the highest glory in virtue of the cross? There is only one explanation possible, namely that it is as MAN that He has been exalted. It is not that as the Son of Man, by inherent right, He has "ascended up where He was before," but that as the Crucified of Calvary He is enthroned in all the glory of God.

And this may explain what to some may seem a difficulty. The Apostle John was not only "the disciple whom He

[19]Philippians 3:21.
[20]I John 3:2.
[21]Philippians 2:8,9, R.V.
[22]John 17:5.

loved"—he was one of the favored three who were with Him on the Mount of Transfiguration; how is it, then, that while that vision of glory served only to excite wondering worship, and led the disciples to pray for its continuance,[23] he was so completely overwhelmed by the vision of the Lord vouchsafed to him at Patmos? "When I saw Him," he writes, "I fell at His feet as dead." May not the explanation be that, whereas the glory of "the Holy Mount" was that of "the Son of man coming in his kingdom,"[24] the Patmos vision revealed Him in all the fulness of the supreme glory to which He was exalted when "begotten again from the dead"? He was "like unto the Son of Man"; but "His eyes were as a flame of fire." "And he had in his right hand seven stars; and out of his mouth went a sharp two-edged sword, and his countenance was as the sun shineth in his strength."[25]

And it is as thus exalted that the Christian is called upon to know Him and to worship Him. It is not that there are many Christs, but that "upon His head are many crowns." Nor is it that the Lord Jesus of Bethlehem and Calvary is lost to us. "He laid His right hand upon me, saying unto me, Fear not," is the seer's record of the scene when he lay like one dead in presence of such awful glory. But though his hand held the stars of that vision of glory, it was the same loving hand that had so often rested on him in the days of the humiliation. And though that voice was "as the sound of many waters," the words were such as the beloved disciple was doubtless used to hear during the ministry of the forty days—"I am he that liveth, and was dead; and, behold, I am alive for evermore, Amen; and have the keys of hell and of death" (Rev. 1:18).

[23]"Lord, it is good for us to be here" (Matt. 17:4).
[24]The division of the chapters obscures the connection between Matthew 16:28 and the record of the Transfiguration.
[25]Revelation 1:14, 16.

That supreme glory was His, I repeat, by inherent right. "Originally in the form of God," and "on an equality with God," are the words of the often-cited text. But, not counting this "a prize" (or "a thing to be grasped"), He emptied Himself—divested Himself of it all.[26]

The inference of the rationalistic "Higher Criticism" is that during His earthly sojourn He was, in effect, a mere man, and therefore a dupe of the ignorance and error which prevailed among the Jews of His time. And this, moreover, not merely in ordinary matters, but in the sphere that most vitally concerned His ministry and His mission.[27] Strange it is that even unspiritual men can fail to be shocked by the profanity of this; stranger still that even a surface acquaintance with the Gospels does not enable them to detect its falseness. For the antithesis so often emphasized in His teaching was not between the divine and the human, but between the Father and the Son.

Nor was this the limit of His self-renunciation. He not merely "emptied Himself" in coming into the world, but, "being found in fashion as a man He humbled Himself." And yet He claimed to forgive sins, and to be Lord of the Sabbath and in the hour of what seemed His greatest weakness and shame He declared that He could summon myriads of angels to His help.[28]

Is this the attitude, is this the language, of "a Jew of His time"? As we read the record we realize that we are in the divine presence of the Son of Man. And yet He humbled

[26]Philippians 2:6, 7. (See R.V., margin.)

[27]Here are the words of the standard textbook of the cult: "Christ . . . held the current Jewish notions respecting the divine authority and revelation of the Old Testament." (Hasting's *Bible Dict.*, article "Old Testament," p. 601.)

[28]"But," He added, as with divine knowledge He surveyed the wide field of the prophetic Scriptures, "how then shall the Scriptures be fulfilled?" (Matt. 26:53, 54).

Himself to the extent of giving up even His liberty as a man, and refraining, not merely from doing His own will, but even from speaking His own words.

The holiest of men could not be trusted thus. When, in His dealings with the exiles of the Captivity, God needed a prophet who would never speak save in words divinely given, He struck Ezekiel dumb. Two judgments had already fallen on the nation—first, the Servitude, and then the Captivity, to Babylon. But they were warned that, if they remained impenitent, a third, more terrible than either, would befall them—that of the seventy years' Desolations; and until the day when Jerusalem, their boast and pride, was smitten, Ezekiel's mouth was closed, save when the Spirit came unto him, and God gave him words to speak.[29] But the self-renunciation of the Son of God was so absolute and unreserved that He could use language such as this:

"The Son can do nothing of himself, but what he seeth the Father do" (John 5:19).

"He that rejecteth me, and receiveth not my words, hath one that judgeth him: the word that I have spoken, the same shall judge him in the last day. For I have not spoken of myself; but the Father which sent me, he gave me a commandment, what I should say, and what I should speak. And I know that his commandment is life everlasting: whatsoever I speak, therefore, even as the Father said unto me, so I speak" (John 12:48-50).

Are these the words of One who "held the current Jewish notions" of His time? Blind though they were, the Jews of His time were not so blind as some *Christian* ministers and professors of *Christian* Universities today. For the Jews could recognize that "He taught them as one having authority, and not as their scribes."[30] From the scribes they were

---

[29]Ezekiel 3:26, 27; 24:24-27; 33:21, 22.
[30]Matthew 7:29.

used to receiving definite and dogmatic teaching, but it was teaching based upon "the law and the prophets": here was One who stood apart and taught them from a wholly different plane. The words of the Apostles and Evangelists were "inspired," but His words were "the words of God"[31] in a higher sense. For it was not merely the body of His teaching that was thus divine, but the very language in which it was conveyed. So that in His prayer on the betrayal night He could say not only "I have given them thy word," but "I have given them the *words* which thou gavest me."[32]

So complete was His self-renunciation and submission that beyond what the Father gave Him to speak He knew nothing, and was silent. With reference to His coming in glory, for instance, He declared, "Of that day or that hour knoweth no one, not even the angels in heaven, neither the Son, but the Father."[33]

This was not within His "authority"; the Father had not given Him to speak of it. But if and when He spoke, He spoke with authority. "Whatsoever I speak, therefore," He declared, "even as the Father said unto me, so I speak."[34] What wonder, then, that He said again—and the words gain tremendous force from being part of the very same sentence in which He disclaimed the knowledge of the time of His return—"Heaven and earth shall pass away, but my words shall not pass away."[35] What wonder that He declared His coming to be the crisis of the world!

---

[31]John 3:34.
[32]John 17:8, 14.
[33]Mark 13:22 (and Matt. 24:36, R.V.).
[34]John 12:50.
[35]Mark 13:31.

4

THE SON OF GOD

WE HAVE seen, then, that "the Son of Man" is a Messianic title only in the sense that it belongs to Him who is Israel's Messiah; further, that the Lord assumed this higher glory when His Messianic claims were rejected; and lastly, that so far from its implying sonship by a human father, the title is altogether independent of His human birth. He was not only the man who was born in Bethlehem, but the Son of Man who "descended out of heaven"—Man by a higher title than human birth could give.

In speaking of Him as the man of Bethlehem and Nazareth we are treading, as it were, the sacred enclosure reserved for the feet of the covenant people. And when we dwell upon His glory as the Son of Man, we seem to have passed the outer veil, where none but anointed priests might enter. But He is not merely the Son of Man, but the Son of God; and here we stand before the second veil which shrouds the mysteries of the holiest of all.

And if we may dare to draw aside that veil, let us take heed that we do so with befitting reverence, and in the spirit of the words of Agur's "prophecy." We do well to recall them here: "Who hath ascended up into heaven, or descended? . . . What is his name, and what is his Son's name, if thou canst tell? . . . *Add thou not unto his words.*"[1] Here, then, are some of the words of the Son of God: "All things have been delivered unto me of my Father; and no one knoweth the Son, save the Father.[2]

[1]Proverbs 30:4, 6.
[2]Matthew 11:27.

The Lord goes on to say, "Neither doth any know the Father save the Son, and *he to whomsoever the Son willeth to reveal him*";[3] but there is no such added clause respecting the knowledge of the Son. No ONE KNOWETH THE SON, SAVE THE FATHER; or, as the Lord expressed it upon another occasion more definitely still,[4] "No one knoweth *who the Son is*, save the Father." This is absolute, and in the light of it we read the Apostle's words, "the mystery of God, even Christ."[5]

Would that this had always been remembered in the past! For the truth of Christ has suffered more from the mistaken zeal of its learned and devout defenders, than from the ignorance and malice of its assailants, heretical or profane. There are truths which we can make our own, and these we can distribute, so to speak, in our own image. But in presence of truth so solemn, so mysterious, so transcendental, it is our part simply to accept what is written, and to keep to the very words in which it is revealed.

An incident in the French Chamber might teach us a lesson here, for "the children of this world are wiser in their generation than the children of light." Trouble was caused in a certain district through the general in command having communicated a War Office order in his own words. And when the Minister of War was challenged in Parliament for punishing him, his answer was, "He committed an offence, and I removed him; he paraphrased an order which it was his duty only to read."

---

[3]The popular belief that men by nature know the Father is in direct opposition to these explicit words of the Lord Jesus Christ.
[4]Luke 10:22. Here Dean Alford writes, "I am convinced that our Lord did utter, *on the two separate occasions*, these weighty words." And Alford's proverbial intolerance of "harmonizing or escaping difficulties" lends weight to his judgment on such a point.
[5]Colossians 2:2, R.V.

And men have offended grievously by paraphrasing the words in which "the mystery of God" has been revealed. The Sonship of Christ has thus been defined and explained in the terms used to express the generation of human beings, thus affording the Jew a further excuse for his unbelief, and the Moslem an occasion for his blasphemies. As the Lord's title of Son of Man does not mean that He was begotten by a man, but that He is the very impersonation of humanity, ought we not to interpret His title of Son of God on this same principle?

But is He not called the "only *begotten* Son of God"? Such is indeed the inaccurate rendering of our English versions.[6] Etymologically "onlybegotten," as one word, would be the precise equivalent in English of the Greek word here used (monogenes); but what concerns us is not the etymology of the word, but the meaning of it.

The language of the New Testament is largely based upon that of the Greek version of the Old; and this word is used by the LXX. to represent a Hebrew term of endearment—a term in which there is no suggestion whatever of "begetting." It properly denotes "only"; and by a natural transition it comes to mean *unique,* and then *greatly beloved.*

In six of its twelve occurrences the Septuagint Version has "beloved," the very word by which the Lord Jesus was hailed from heaven at His baptism, and again on the Holy Mount. And in every one of these six passages our English translators render it "only." In one passage (Ps. 68:6), it is taken, both in the Greek Bible and also in the English, to mean "solitary"; and in Proverbs 4:3 it is rendered by a term of affection.

[6]"This rendering somewhat obscures the exact sense of the original word. . . . The thought in the original is centered in the personal Being of the Son, and not in His generation." (Bishop Westcott in "The Speaker's Com.," John 14.)

In the four remaining passages (Judges 11:34; Ps. 22:20; 25:16; and 35:17), the Septuagint rendering is *monogenes*. The first of these passages tells us that Jephthah's daughter was his *only* child. In Psalm 25 the word in our translations is "desolate." And in Psalms 22 and 35, where our divine Lord is referred to as, "darling" is the word used in the English versions.

Then as to the use of this word monogenes in the New Testament; in three of the nine passages where it occurs, it means an *only* child (Luke 7:12; 8:42; 9:38). And their rendering of it by "only begotten" in Hebrews 11:17 suggests that our translators regarded this English phrase as a term of endearment; for Isaac, though his father's darling, was not his only son. In the other passages where it occurs, it designates the Son of God (John 1:14, 18; 3:16, 18; and I John 4:9).

The view we take of the first of these passages will influence our reading of the rest. "And we beheld his glory, glory as of the only begotten from the Father." Thus the revisers have given a literal translation of the text. And apart from controversy, every one would naturally understand it to mean that the glory of Christ was glory such as the Father would bestow upon the only Son. But yet most commentators read it differently, although the phrase "only begotten *from* the Father" is as unusual in Greek as it is in English, and the meaning of the word rendered "only begotten" is acknowledged to be "only" and "beloved."[7]

---

[7]Grimm's Lexicon gives it "single of its kind, only"; and adds, "He is so spoken of by John, not because of generation by God, but because He is of nature, or essentially, Son of God."

Dean Alford says: "In New Testament usage it signifies the *only* Son." ("Gr. Test. Com.")

Bloomfield says, with reference to "the Beloved" in Ephesians 1:6:

Such, indeed, is clearly the governing thought in every passage where the word is applied to the Lord; and it may be averred with confidence that, but for the controversies of other days, no other element would have been imported into it. "Words are the counters of wise men, the money of fools," and in this sphere, above all others, it behooves us to keep clear of folly. The meaning of a word is settled by its use, and having regard to the Scriptural use of the word here in question, it is certain that the dogma with which it is associated must be based on some other foundation. And to base it on His title of "Son" is, as we have seen, to ignore the meaning of that word in Scriptural usage.

But it may be demanded, How then is His Sonship to be explained? The mysteries of the Christian revelation have this in common with the superstitious dogmas that have been based upon it, that they claim acceptance on transcendental grounds. But here the analogy ends; for although these truths of revelation may be above our reason, yet, unlike the errors of superstition, they never outrage reason. But while with the "Christian religionist" "the voice of the Church" is an end of controversy, and he refuses to discuss the dogmas of his creed, the Christian seems to have so little confidence in the Word of God that he is always eager to "explain" the mysteries of his faith.

A signal example of the evil of this tendency is afforded by the usual perversion of the Apostle Paul's defense of the

---

"It may be compared with *monogenes* of John 1:14, 18, 3:18; I John 4:9, where the full sense is 'only and most dearly beloved.' " ("Gr. Test. Com.")

And the crowning proof is the marginal reading of John 1:18, in the R.V., "God only begotten." This reading, which has high MS. authority, would be in the text of the R.V. if Westcott and Hort had had their way. Dr. Hort's "Dissertation" on the subject, read at Cambridge in 1876, is the most thorough defense of it. But I refer to it only as a proof that *monogenes* does not mean "Begotten."

resurrection. In reply to the demand, "How are the dead raised up, and with what body do they come?" he does not attempt to *explain* the mystery. His answer is, "Thou fool!" The words which follow are the germ and "pattern" of Bishop Butler's great "apology."[8] If, the Apostle argues, we cannot explain the most familiar processes of Nature—as, for instance, the growth of corn from "bare grain," dead and buried in the ground—how can we expect to explain the resurrection of the dead?

But if there be a living God—an Almighty God—there is no improbability in the thought of the resurrection. And so, when arraigned before his heathen judges at Cæsarea, the Apostle exclaimed, "Why should it be thought a thing incredible with you that God should raise the dead?" And in the same spirit we may well demand, Why should it be thought a thing incredible that God should manifest Himself to men? For if we recognize, as all thoughtful persons must recognize, the reasonableness of such a revelation,[9] the only question open relates to the manner of it.

And judging by our Bible "Dictionaries" and "Encyclopædias," it would seem that our decision of that question should depend on whether the divine method commends itself to the "wise and prudent." That God thundered forth His law at Sinai, and engraved it upon stone, the "wise and prudent" scout as a superstitious legend. And that "His only begotten Son declared Him," they reject as mysticism.

If, indeed, instead of living in a remote province, and among a superstitious people—they happened to be the land and people of the Covenant!—the Christ had submitted His claims to committees of scientific experts in Rome and Athens, and the "blue-book" containing their report upon His test

[8]"The Analogy of Religion with the Constitution and Course of Nature."
[9]As has been justly said, "The idea of a revelation may be said to be logically involved in the notion of a living God" (Fairburn).

miracles were before them, the "wise and prudent" would believe in Him. But Christians are so dull-witted that even if such a blue-book were available they would prefer the New Testament! And in the New Testament they find that when, during His ministry, the "wise and prudent" rejected Him, He "answered and said, I thank Thee, O Father, Lord of heaven and earth, because Thou hast hid these things from the wise and prudent, and hast revealed them unto babes."

"Babes"—that is, children.[10] It is not that children are unintelligent—they are often more quick-witted than their seniors—but that they are guileless, and believe what they are told. And if in this spirit we enter on the study of the Bible, we shall be content to accept the divine revelation about Christ, without attempting to explain its mysteries. But we are not content to take the place of children. And the result is deplorable. For just as the mysteries of the Atonement are "explained" in the language of the market and the criminal court, so the mysteries of the Incarnation are "explained" in the language of—!

But here I check myself.[11] I am not unmindful that it is only the unlearned who base His title of Son of God upon the Virgin birth. But the majority of Christians are "unlearned." The first occurrence in the New Testament of the full title, the "Son of God," is the Apostle Peter's confession:[12] "Thou art the Christ, the Son of the living God." Was this confession due to a sudden appreciation of the fact that the Lord's mother was a virgin? The suggestion is both painful and grotesque.[13] That could be attested by "flesh and blood"

[10]It is the word used in I Corinthians 13:11; Galatians 4:3; Ephesians 4:14.

[11]The subject is a delicate one; I deal with it in an Appendix note.

[12]Matthew 16:16. See p. 40 *ante.*, App. note.

[13]Quite as painful, and still more grotesque, would be the suggestion that this was the burden of Paul's preaching in the Damascus synagogues (Acts 9:20).

on the recognized principles of evidence;[14] but of this truth of His Sonship the Lord declared, "Flesh and blood hath not revealed it unto thee, but My Father which is in heaven."

And so was it with all the Eleven at the last; throughout His ministry He had been subjected to a constant ordeal of interrogation. But His words at the Supper drew from them the confession, "Now we are sure that thou knowest all things, and needest not that any one should question thee; by this we believe that thou camest forth from God."[15] It was not what He had become in virtue of His human birth, but what He was by inherent right. For His "coming forth from God" does not point to the manger of Bethlehem, and the date of the Nativity, but to a past Eternity and the Father's throne.

And this is the truth on which the faith of the Christian rests—the faith that "overcometh the world." "For whosoever shall confess that Jesus is the Son of God, God dwelleth in him, and he in God."[16] It is not an inference from the Virgin birth, but a revelation from the Father in heaven.

If, then, His title of Son of God does not depend on the Virgin birth—and it is a fact of vital moment that the word "begotten" is used of Him only in relation to His resurrection from the dead[17]—what can be its significance? The only meaning that can be given to it is that which it conveyed to those who heard His teaching, those among whom He lived and died. Just as by "Son of Man" He claimed to be man in the highest and most absolute sense, so by "Son of God"

[14]That the mother of our Lord was a virgin is stated in the Gospel narrative as plain matter of fact. But the "wise and prudent" seem to be ignorant of the strict and elaborate provisions of the Jewish law for testing the virginity of brides.

[15]John 16:30.

[16]I John 4:15.

[17]Psalm 2:7; Acts 13:33.

See App. note, p. 107 *post.*

He laid claim to Deity. His disciples understood it thus, and they worshipped Him as divine; and those who refused to believe in Him understood it thus, and they crucified Him as a blasphemer.

5

THE TESTIMONY OF MATTHEW

THE GOSPELS may be studied either as the divinely accredited records of the Ministry, or as a progressive revelation of Christ. Not that the Lord's teaching was divided chronologically into sections, but that in the books which contain the inspired record of His teaching there is a definite and systematic "progress of doctrine." The purpose of the First Gospel, for example, is to record His Messianic mission to the people of the covenant, and it contains nothing save what relates to that mission. A fuller spiritual knowledge of Scripture is needed, perhaps, to enable us to recognize in Mark the revelation of Him as Jehovah's Servant; but no one can miss the prominence which the humanity of Christ holds in the Third Gospel; and the distinctive character of the Fourth, as the revelation of the Son of God, is universally acknowledged.

But though the Gospels thus present us with four different portraits, there is but one Christ. And while the Fourth Gospel was written expressly to reveal Him as the Son of God, it displays Him none the less as Israel's Messiah, Jehovah's Servant, and the Son of Man. For such is the divine system of a progressive revelation. What has yet to be unfolded is rarely anticipated, but what has been already revealed is incorporated and continued.

"He came unto his own, and his own received him not."[1] This brief sentence on the opening page of the Fourth Gospel sums up the story of His Messianic mission as recorded

---

[1] John 1:11. Here our English idiom fails; the French is admirable: "Il est venu chez soi, et les siens ne l'ont point recu."

in the First. And when we read that "The Word was made flesh, and dwelt among us," we recall the Virgin birth. No need to set forth the manner of it, for that has been already told, and now all that remains is to give the full revelation of the Son of God.

Not even the full title, "the Son of God,"[2] is to be found in the earlier Gospels, save only in Peter's confession,[3] in the mysterious homage accorded Him by demons,[4] and in the charge on which the Sanhedrin condemned Him for blasphemy. That charge gave proof that He had used it in His ministry. But the Holy Spirit, in inspiring the records of the Ministry, reserved the unfolding of it for the Apostle whose peculiar receptivity led to his being known among his brethren as the disciple whom He loved. And the purpose of his Gospel is expressly stated at the close: "That ye might believe that Jesus is the Christ, the Son of God"; that "Jesus," the Man who was born in Bethlehem, is the Christ—Israel's Messiah—and that He is the Son of God.

But though the Gospel of John has thoroughly distinctive characteristics, it is merely an advance in a progressive revelation, and not, as some would tell us, a breaking away from all that has gone before. The figment that the other Evangelists do not teach the Deity of Christ betrays extraordinary blindness; for though that truth is nowhere asserted by them as a dogma, it is in the warp and woof of their record of the Lord's ministry. Abundant proof of this may be found in each of the earlier Gospels, but for the present purpose an appeal to the Gospel of Matthew will suffice.

---

[2]See App. note, p. 107 *post*.
[3]Matthew 16:16.
[4]Mark 3:11, Luke 4:41. "Mysterious" I call it, because it cannot have been prompted by Satan, and it was rendered at a time when even His own disciples were only groping after the truth.

Take, for example, the "Sermon on the Mount." Of the Ten Commandments Moses declared, "These words the Lord spake in the Mount, out of the midst of the fire, of the cloud, and of the thick darkness, with a great voice; and *He added no more.*"[5] In Scripture they have a special solemnity. What, then, was the Lord's attitude toward them? "Ye have heard that it was said to them of old time, Thou shalt not kill; but *I say unto you . . .*" And this formula is five times repeated.[6] Was it that He thus intended either to revoke or to disparage the law of Sinai? Far from it; the words are prefaced by the declaration that that law is eternal. But the "Mount of the Beatitudes" spoke with the same divine authority as the mount of the thunder and the fire: this is the explanation of His words.

The Hebrew prophets spake from God, but "Thus saith the Lord" prefaced all their utterances. And though the Apostle Paul had abundant revelations, and he insisted that his words had divine authority, the authority he claimed for them was that they were "commandments of the Lord." He himself was nothing, and the emphatic *ego's* in his teaching are rare; they are usually inserted, indeed, to mark his insignificance. In Colossians, for instance, that wonderful Epistle in which the revelation of the Christ reaches its highest development—there is never an *ego* anywhere, save in declaring himself a servant.[7] But in the Lord's teaching the *ego* stands out with the utmost prominence, and "*I* say unto you" takes the place of "Thus saith the Lord."

Of the law of Sinai He declared, "*Till heaven and earth pass,* one jot or one tittle shall in no wise pass from the law

---

[5]Deuteronomy 5:22.

[6]Matthew 5:22, 28, 34, 39, 44.

[7]Colossians 1:23, 25. There is not another *ego* in the Epistle. The English reader must bear in mind that in Greek the pronoun is ordinarily implied in the verb. It is expressed only where it is emphatic.

till all be fulfilled"; of His own teaching He declared, "Heaven and earth *shall pass away,* but *My words shall not pass away.* "Thou shalt not kill," "Thou shalt not commit adultery," "Thou shalt not steal,"—these are words for *sinners.* And when the great *telos*[8] comes, when all things have been subdued for Him, and God has become all in all—when "the first heaven and the first earth *are* passed away, and the tabernacle of God is with men, and God Himself shall be with them"—then the words of Sinai shall be a memory of an evil past; but the words of the Ministry of our glorious Lord and Saviour shall live as the everlasting heritage of His people.

Entirely in keeping with this is His teaching recorded in the eleventh chapter. Upbraiding the cities wherein most of His mighty works were done, He declared that it shall be more tolerable for Sodom in the day of judgment than for Capernaum. What Sodom was—that name of infamy—we know. But what had Capernaum done? He did mighty works there; He taught in its streets; He made His home in it—it is called "His own city": all this gives proof that in Capernaum there can have been no open hostility to His ministry. But "they repented not"—that is all. Sodom poured contempt upon "the moral law," which was afterwards embodied in the "ten words" thundered forth at Sinai: Capernaum failed to repent on hearing the words of Christ. And yet He declared that the sin of Capernaum was deeper than the flagrant and filthy iniquities of Sodom. If His words were not as divine as the words of Sinai, the profanity of this would be astounding.

---

[8]I Corinthians 15:24. The *telos* in Greek is not the *end* in the sense of our English word. It connotes, not cessation, but result. The *end* of a journey is our arrival at our destination; its *telos* is the accomplishment of the purpose with which we set out.

And yet then and there He owned His position of dependence and subjection, calling upon God as His Father and the Lord of heaven and earth. The most absolute subjection, here and always; but *subordination,* never by word or act throughout His ministry. Notice the terms in which He addresses Him—"Lord of heaven and earth": *His* "Lord" He never calls Him.

And mark what follows. Though He was "the First-born of all creation"—the One by whom and for whom all created things were made; the Word who in the beginning, and before there was a creature made, was with God, and was God[9]—He had, when coming into the world, divested Himself of all His rights and all His glory; but the response of the Father was to re-invest Him with all that He had surrendered. Not, as the Neo-theology would tell us, after His return to heaven—till then, indeed, He could not re-assume *the glory*—but here, in the time and scene of His humiliation and rejection, He could say, "All things are delivered unto Me of My Father." And in the same breath He adds, anticipating the craving which such words excite to understand the mystery of His personality, "No one knoweth the Son, save the Father."

And then—"Come unto Me, all ye that labor and are heavy laden, and *I* will give you rest." Another emphatic *I.* If words like these came from the greatest, holiest, best of men, we should fling them back with indignation. But they are the words of Him by whom and for whom we were created; of Him who spoke from Sinai, and knows the guilt and penalty of sin; of Him to whom all judgment has been committed, and who can anticipate the decrees of the Great Day; of Him—let us not forget it—who "took part of flesh and blood," and knows our burdens and our toils. And when

---

[9]John 1:1-3.

spiritual men dwell upon His words, with thoughts like these filling their hearts, they do not sit down to frame a christology; they cast themselves at His feet and worship Him.

Many another passage might be cited, pointing to the same conclusion. "I will build my Church";[10] "Where two or three are gathered together in my name, there am *I* in the midst";[11] "Behold *I* send unto you prophets"[12]—two more of these great, emphatic *ego's,* that would savor of profanity if the speaker were not divine.

When we come to "the Second Sermon on the Mount"— chapters 24 and 25—the same conclusion is irresistible. There is no "Thus saith the Lord" to accredit His words, as He surveys the great drama of the future, and fixes the course of events, and the destinies of men. As we have seen, He never speaks of God as *His* Lord, but yet, once and again, He here claims to be the Lord of the people of God. If we did not know Him as "our great God and Saviour," this would be quite incomprehensible, if it did not seem utterly profane.

The concluding verses of the First Gospel record the words He spoke on the Galilean mountain which He had appointed as the trystingplace for His disciples after His resurrection from the dead. And it is a strange enigma that any one who accepts the record as Holy Scripture can deny or doubt His Deity. He must have a mind that is not governed by reason. Who can this be who has "all power in heaven and on earth"? Who is this who commissions the disciples to teach *His* commandments? Who is this that dismisses them with the words, "Lo, *I* am with you all the days, even unto the end of the world"? And this is only the fringe, as it were. That the Father is God, and the Holy

---

[10]Matthew 16:18.
[11]Matthew 18:20.
[12]Matthew 23:34.

Spirit is God, Christian and Jew acknowledge. Who, then, is this who claims equality with both, placing His name with theirs, and taking precedence, as men would say, of the Holy Spirit?

I once had the privilege of meeting the late Dr. Edersheim of Oxford,[13] and in our conversation he impressed on me that, when we bring the truth of "the Trinity" before a Jew, it is to his own Scriptures we should appeal. And to exemplify his words he quoted the middle verses of Isaiah 63. Jehovah, the prophecy declares, became the Saviour of His people. But how? "*The Angel of His presence* saved them." The word to Moses was, "Behold I send an angel before thee. . . . Take ye heed of him and hearken unto his voice; provoke him not, for he will not pardon your transgressions, for my name is in him."[14]

If doubt be possible as to who it is that is here indicated, surely it is dispelled by the terms in which the promise was renewed—"*My* presence shall go with thee."[15] Hence the prophet's words, "the Angel of His presence." And mark what follows: "But they rebelled, and vexed *His Holy Spirit*."[16] Thus we have Jehovah, the Angel of His presence, and His Holy Spirit, as the God of the Covenant people in the Old Testament dispensation; and in the New Testament we have the Father, the Son, and the Holy Spirit. The nomenclature is changed, but it is the same God. Some, indeed, would argue that, because the Son is never so designated in the Old Testament, His personality began with the Incarnation. But the argument if valid would apply also to the Father; for the revelation of "the Father" awaited the coming of

---

13 The author of *The Life and Times of Jesus the Messiah* and *Practical Truths from Elisha* by Kregel Publications (1983).

14Exodus 23:20, 21. Verse 22 is noteworthy; it is the Angel's voice, but it is God who speaks.

15Exodus 33:14.   16Compare the words of Stephen in Acts 7:51.

"the Son."[17] And if they who worship Father, Son, and Spirit are justly chargeable with having *three* gods, all who own the Father and the Holy Spirit are no less open to the taunt of having *two*.

But how can this mystery be explained? It is well to acknowledge plainly and with emphasis that in this matter not only the heresies that distracted the professing Church, in the early centuries, but many of the discussions to which they gave rise, assumed that by searching we can find out God, and know the Almighty to perfection.[18]

The story is told of a meeting in a certain provincial town, at which the local clergy were holding forth on the doctrine of "the Trinity." The fool of the place, whom everybody knew as "Silly Billy," excited amusement by the earnestness with which he plied his pencil; and at the close they asked to see his "notes." The paper showed tokens of laborious effort and many failures, but as the result the following lines could be deciphered—

> "This can Silly Billy see,
> Three in One and One in Three,
> And One of them has died for me."

The poor town fool had got hold of what many who are "wise and prudent" miss!

---

[17]The figure of God's Fatherhood to His people is occasionally used in the Psalms and the Prophets, but *"the* Father" is not to be found in the Old Testament. Christ revealed the Father.
[18]Job 11:7.

6

THE TESTIMONY OF JOHN

AS ALREADY noticed, the four Gospels have been described as so many different portraits of Christ—portraits, not biographies; and the portrait presented to us in the Gospel of John is that of Christ as Son of God. To the intelligent reader its *omissions,* of which unbelief makes much for its evil purposes, afford a striking indication of its Divine authorship, and of the purpose for which it has been given.

The Apostle John is the only one of the four Evangelists who was with the Lord on the Mount of Transfiguration, and yet he is the only one whose Gospel makes no mention of that vision of glory. He is the only one of the Evangelists who witnessed the agony in the Garden, and yet he is the only one whose Gospel is silent with respect to it. And though one of the eleven disciples who were with the Lord on the Mount of Olives when He was "taken up from them into heaven," his book contains never a word of direct record about the Ascension.

May not these extraordinary omissions be explained if we remember that in the vision of the Holy Mount the Lord appeared in His glory as *Son of Man,* whereas the purpose of the Fourth Gospel is to reveal Him as *Son of God.* So also with regard to Gethsemane, we have the Lord's explicit words, "The *Son of Man* is betrayed into the hands of sinners." And though His exaltation to the right hand of God proclaimed Him to be the Son of God, this was beyond the scope of the

Evangelist's commission,[1] for it was of the *earthly* ministry
that He was inspired to write.

But there is another "omission," far more extraordinary
even than these. The writer is the disciple to whom the Lord
in His dying hour entrusted the care of His mother; "and
from that hour," we read, "that disciple took her unto his
own home." What talks they must have had together about
the sacred birth and childhood! What unnumbered hours
he must have spent in listening to her thrilling reminiscences!
And how ineffaceably must the record have been stamped
upon his memory and his heart! And yet not a word is to
be found here about the angel's visit, the Bethlehem inn,
or the home life at Nazareth. "He was in the world." "The
Word was made flesh, and dwelt among us." And that is
all! For though He of whom the Evangelist speaks is the
Man of Bethlehem and Nazareth, yet here again it is not of
Him as *Man* that he is inspired to write, but as the Son of God.

"Inspired," I say again advisedly; for if these omissions
are not to be accounted for by the divine guidance and
restraint that we call "inspiration," what explanation can be
given of them? Put yourself in his place. If any one of
us had had the Apostle John's experiences, is it conceivable
that we could write a book about the Lord without referring
to them? Indeed, if this Gospel be a merely human work,
it presents a psychological phenomenon so extraordinary as
to have no parallel in the literature of the world.

Here are the opening words of it: "In the beginning was
the Word, and the Word was with God, and the Word was
God. The same was in the beginning with God. All things
were made by him; and without him was not any thing

---

[1]The Messianic Gospel—Matthew—also omits the Ascension because
the closing words of it belong *dispensationally* to the time when
Zechariah 14:4 shall be fulfilled (compare Acts 1:11), and Christ will
send out His earthly people as His missionaries to evangelize the world.

made that was made. In him was life; and the life was the light of men" (chapter 1:1-4).

The book was written, we are expressly told, that we might believe that He is the *Son of God*;[2] and it begins by proclaiming that He is God. Could there be a clearer proof of the significance of the title "Son of God"? He is called the "Son of Man" because He is "very man," and He is called the "Son of God" because He is "very God." The book as a whole is designed to confirm faith in His Godhood.

The layman is apt to exaggerate the relative value of direct evidence, but the lawyer recognizes that no testimony is more convincing than that which is incidental; and here, as in the preceding notice of the First Gospel, it is to the indirect and incidental proof that I would briefly claim attention.

To the Christian the positive statement that "the Word was God" seems to be "an end of controversy"; but this statement was used by the Arians to prove that He held a subordinate position.[3] And when the alternative reading of verse 18 ("the only begotten God") was pressed on them, they seized on the words as distinguishing Him from the Father, who alone was God in the highest sense.

The Arian controversy indeed affords signal proof of what has been often noticed, that the Fathers were influenced by the paganism which prevailed around them, and in which so many of them had been steeped before their conversion to Christianity. And to the pagan mind there was nothing

[2] John 20:31.
[3] Critics who take the Arian view urge the absence of the article in the phrase "the Word was God"; but "the writer could not have written it thus without manifest absurdity" (Bishop Middleton), for that would imply that He was God in an exclusive sense. I Timothy 2:5 supplies a parallel; and, following the R.V. reading of it, "one mediator . . . Himself Man," we might here read, "the Word was with God, and the Word was Himself God."

absurd, or even incongruous, in the conception of a subordinate God; whereas to us, who think of God only as the Supreme Being, it involves a contradiction in terms, and seems mere nonsense. With us, therefore, the issue is a definite and simple one, namely, whether Christ is God, or only man.

Let us, then, shake ourselves free from the prejudices which religion seems to excite in the minds of many, and also from the slovenly-mindedness that leads us to give an unthinking assent to truths which, if really believed, would influence our whole life; and, in the spirit of honest and earnest seekers after truth, let us try to grasp the significance of the words of the Lord Jesus as recorded in this book. Here are a few of His sayings, culled almost at random, and from a single section of it:

"I am the bread of life: he that cometh to me shall never hunger, and he that believeth on me shall never thirst" (John 6:35).

"He that believeth on me hath everlasting life: I am the bread of life" (6:47, 48).

"I am the living bread which came down from heaven: if any man eat of this bread, he shall live for ever: and the bread that I will give is my flesh, which I will give for the life of the world" (6:51).

"He that believeth on me, as the scripture hath said, out of his belly shall flow the rivers of living water" (7:38).

"I am the light of the world" (8:12).

"If a man keep my word, he shall never see death" (8:51).

"Before Abraham was, I am" (8:58).

"Therefore doth my Father love me, because I lay down my life, that I may take it again. No one taketh it from me, but I lay it down of myself. I have power to lay it down, and I have power to take it again" (10:17, 18).

"I am the good shepherd. . . . My sheep hear my voice, and I know them, and they follow me; and I give unto them eternal life; and they shall never perish, neither shall any man pluck them out of my hand. . . . I and my Father are one" (10:11, 27, 28, 30).

As we ponder such words as these we seem to be basking in the sunshine, and we are ready to exclaim, as Thomas did, "My Lord and my God." But some of us have minds so constituted that clouds of doubt cover our sky at times, and we ask ourselves, How can we be sure that these are really the very words of Christ? Let us then look at other sayings of His, the genuineness of which is confirmed by facts. The following are His words recorded in John 5:21-29:

"For as the Father raiseth up the dead, and quickeneth them; even so the Son quickeneth whom he will. For the Father judgeth no man, but hath committed all judgment unto the Son; that all men should honour the Son, even as they honour the Father. He that honoureth not the Son, honoureth not the Father which hath sent him. Verily, verily, I say unto you, he that heareth my word, and believeth on him that sent me, hath everlasting life, and shall not come into condemnation; but is passed from death unto life. Verily, verily, I say unto you, The hour is coming, and now is, when the dead shall hear the voice of the Son of God; and they that hear shall live. For as the Father hath life in himself, so hath he given to the Son to have life in himself; and hath given him authority to execute judgment also, because he is the Son of man. Marvel not at this: for the hour is coming, in the which all that are in the graves shall hear his voice, and shall come forth; they that have done good, unto the resurrection of life, and they that have done evil, unto the resurrection of damnation."

The Lord here unequivocally claims equal honor with God the Father. He declares that as the Father raises the dead, so He Himself "gives life to whom He will." He has life *in Himself*: not life derived or delegated, but life as God has life. And He adds that it will be at *His* command that the graves shall yet give up their dead.

What meaning shall we give to such words as these? The narrative of the eleventh chapter supplies the answer; for there we read that, standing by a tomb which covered a decaying corpse, "He cried with a loud voice, Lazarus, come forth; and he that was dead came forth."

Martha's halting faith could credit Him with power to save her brother's life. She held, moreover, a conventional belief in "the resurrection at the last day." But she was utterly incapable of grasping the truth or meaning of His words, "*I* am the resurrection and the life"; and so, when He directed the opening of the grave, she at once exclaimed, "Lord, by this time he stinketh, for he hath been dead four days." "Said I not unto thee," was the Lord's gracious rebuke, "that if thou wouldest believe, thou shouldest see the glory of God?" And then and there she had a vision of that glory, for in obedience to His word, "he that was dead came forth."

People who reject the divine direction implied in inspiration may reasonably doubt the accuracy of a record of spoken words. But this is a narrative of facts. The writer here gives a detailed account of events which happened before his eyes. Lazarus of Bethany he knew personally. And he saw him come out of his grave in obedience to the call of Christ, "bound hand and foot with grave-clothes." The casuistry of skepticism may belittle the account of miracles of another kind, but here is a cause in which mistake was impossible. Unless the whole story be a fabrication—and in that case the writer was a profane impostor—the resurrection of Lazarus is a fact. And if the resurrection is a fact, "the riddle of the universe" is solved: God, "the author and giver of life," has manifested Himself to men. The Deity of Christ is established.

The Rationalist is too intelligent not to recognize this; and so, "to save his face," he rejects the Fourth Gospel. But if any one who professes to believe the Scriptures denies or questions the Deity of Christ, he not only belies his Christian profession, but outrages reason itself. For none but God could give life to a decaying corpse.

But it may be said, perhaps, the Apostle Peter called Dorcas back to life, and notable miracles were wrought by the other Apostles also. Yes, and this would in itself be proof of the Deity of the Lord Jesus; for it was in His name that all their mighty works were done. In His name: not in the name of the Father, but of the Son. When the Apostle Paul declared that he was in no respect "behind the very chiefest Apostles," he added, *though I be nothing.*" And to his amazing boast, "I can do *all things,*" he added, "through Christ who strengthens me." In himself he had no power. But here is One who not only has power in Himself, but who can empower others to act in His name. And He has life in Himself—life in the sense in which none but God has life, so that He can say "*I am the life.*"

But, it may be asked, was not His prayer at the grave of Lazarus an acknowledgment of His dependence on the Father? Dependence, yes; but not in the sense of incompetence or weakness, but of entire submission. That prayer is to be read in the light of His words, "I do nothing of Myself." Though He could say, "The Son giveth me to whom He will," that power and that will were held in absolute subjection to the will of the Father.

7

THE TESTIMONY OF JAMES AND HEBREWS

"JAMES, a servant of God, and of the Lord Jesus Christ, to the twelve tribes which are of the dispersion, greeting" (Jas. 1:1).

It is almost impossible for a Gentile Christian to appreciate the amazing change in the mind and heart of a devout Jew which words like these betoken. Though sects and heresies were many in Judaism, the great truth of the One God was held with passionate fervor by all, whether orthodox or heretic; and yet here the Deity of Christ is unequivocally acknowledged[1] by one who in the course of the Ministry had shared the prevailing unbelief.[2]

Superstition pictures the Christ of the Ministry with a halo round His head, and skepticism represents Him as echoing "current Jewish notions."[3] But while the Christian worships Him as Divine, he recalls the words of the prophet, "He hath no form nor comeliness, and when we shall see Him there is no beauty that we should desire Him." And yet, even with Isaiah 53 in view, no Gentile Christian perhaps can understand how a Jew regarded the Lord and His ministry. "There was in such a Messiah absolutely nothing—past, present, or possible; intellectually, religiously, or even nationally—to attract, but all to repel."

---

[1]This is so, whether the sentence be construed epexigetically or read as in our English Versions. That a Jew could bracket a fellow-man with the God of Israel in this way is quite incredible.
[2]John 7:5. [3]See p. 35, *ante*.

This startling dictum of Dr. Edersheim's[4] may help us to appreciate the testimony of the Epistle of James. The truth of the Deity of Christ must have been forced upon the writer by overwhelmingly compelling proofs. And as that truth is assumed without a word of "apology" or explanation, it must have been accepted by all the Jewish believers, for it was to them that the Epistle was addressed.

"James, the Lord's brother," is the only New Testament writer who never names Him otherwise than as *Lord*. He names Him indeed only once again, when he writes, "My brethren, hold not the faith of our Lord Jesus Christ, the Lord of glory, with respect of persons" (Jas. 2:1). Is it conceivable that a man with the training of a Jew could write such a sentence, unless He believed that Christ was Divine? And it is a fact of extreme significance that throughout his Epistle he uses this title, "the Lord," indifferently of both the Father and the Son.[5] And his testimony ought to have increased weight with those who regard the writer as a "Judaiser."

But I would enter a protest in passing against the disparagement of this Epistle by certain of the Fathers and Reformers. The current theology of Christendom regards the present dispensation as the climax of God's purposes of blessing for earth; but the New Testament represents it as an episode, filling up the interval between the setting aside of the Covenant people and their restoration again to favor. During that interval the Church, the body of Christ, is being gathered out; and the Church in its lower aspect, as a public organization upon earth, ought, according to the divine pur-

[4]"Life and Times of the Messiah," vol. 1 p. 145.
[5]See, e.g., verses 7, 8, 10, 11, 14, 15, of James 5. The Greek *Kurios* has as wide a range of meaning as our word "Lord." It is sometimes used as a mere title of dignity, equivalent to the English "Sir," and at other times it denotes the Supreme Being. In the Greek Bible it is the rendering for "Jehovah." Its force in this Epistle is not doubtful.

pose, to fill the place which the Covenant people were intended to hold. But through the apostasy of Christendom the main channel has become a stagnant pool; and the professing Church as a whole has lapsed from the place originally assigned to it.

With us today all this is elementary truth, but the Fathers had but a very partial apprehension of it, and the German Reformers shared their ignorance. What specially concerns us here, however, is that in the transitional Pentecostal dispensation, recorded in the Acts of the Apostles, the Jew still held a distinctive place. And while "to the Jew, first," characterized it throughout, "to the Jew *only*" marked its initial phase. And it is to that period that the Epistle of James should be assigned, and to that dispensation his ministry specially pertained.[6]

It is just because the Pentecostal Church was Jewish that in considering the indirect evidence for the Deity of Christ, the belief of the early disciples is of such importance. For it is inconceivable that these Jewish converts could have come to worship two Gods, and yet the Epistles that were specially their own make it clear that their belief in Christ as God was outside the sphere of controversy or doubt.

---

[6]I here assume that the James of the Epistle was "the Lord's brother"; for the study of many a treatise to prove the contrary has satisfied me that he held that relationship. Indeed Matthew 13:55 is conclusive. The ordinary "man-of-the-world" Jew knew nothing of a "pre-existent divine Messiah." The Christ he looked for was one of his own people, and therefore that he should have cousins would be regarded as a matter of course—they supposed that John the Baptist was the Christ (Luke 3:15); but the thought of His having brothers and sisters seems to have been repugnant to him.

And a careful study of the chronological question has convinced me that they are right who hold the Epistle of James to be perhaps the earliest of the New Testament writings. It belongs to that period of the Pentecostal dispensation when the whole Church was Jewish, and when their meeting-places still bore the Jewish designation of "synagogues" (James 2:2).

To many the testimony of the Epistle to the Hebrews may seem more telling in this respect than that of James, although here we cannot appeal with certainty to the personality of the writer. No one who has experience in dealing with questions of the kind will ignore either the weighty evidence which connects the Apostle Paul with the Epistle, or the difficulties which beset the hypothesis of his authorship. When dealing in a practical way with such problems, the expert often finds in some purely incidental point a clew to the way out of a seeming *impasse*. And here a sentence in the typically "Pauline" postscript to the Epistle may possibly suggest the solution of this much-debated question. "Suffer the word of exhortation," the writer concludes, "for I have written a letter unto you *in few words.*"

This is generally dismissed as a meaningless conventionalism, for Hebrews is one of the longest of the Epistles; and moreover, as has been often noticed, the first twelve chapters are a treatise rather than an Epistle. And as it is to the thirteenth chapter that the advocates of the Pauline hypothesis specially appeal, may not that last chapter contain the "few words" added by the great Apostle in sending the treatise to those for whom it was written?[7]

But whatever view we take of its authorship, the testimony which the Epistle renders to the Lord's Deity is conclusive. Even if we dismiss every question of inspiration, and regard it merely as a human work, it proves beyond doubt that the doctrine of the Godhood held rank at that time among the certainties of the faith.

Here we need not go beyond the first chapter, or, indeed, the opening sentences of it. By the Son it was that God

[7]This is not a theory hastily formed for the purpose of my "argument," but a belief which I have held for many years. A statement of the grounds on which it is based would require a lengthy excursus that would not be germane to the subject of these pages.

made the worlds. He is the effulgence of the glory of God, and the impress, or very image, of the Person of God. And He it is who upholds all things by the word of His power. If all this applies to a creature, words have no meaning, and "Christian doctrine" may be dismissed as a tangle of hyperbole and superstition. And if the Son be not a creature, he must be God. No pagan alternative can be accepted by either Christian or Jew.

And this disposes of that subtle phase of error which ascribes a kind of secondary Divinity to the Son, while refusing to recognize His Deity. Appeal is made to numerous passages which represent God as working by and through the Son, whether in the sphere of creation, or of government, or of redemption. And stress is laid on the emphatic statement that "to us there is one God, the Father, of whom are all things, and we unto Him, and one Lord, Jesus Christ, through whom are all things, and we through Him." But if the Socinian reads these words aright, then, in view of the uncompromising monotheism of Scripture, we must relegate our Lord and Saviour to the position of a fellow-creature; and to pay Him any divine homage whatever is pagan idolatry, and treason against God.

The prominent place which this difficulty has occupied in all the controversies of all the centuries is proof of its reality and its magnitude. But it is to be solved, not by giving up Christianity, but by accepting the plain and emphatic words of our Lord Jesus Christ, by which He declares His oneness with the Father—words such as these

"I and my Father are one" (John 10:30).

"The Father is in me, and I in him" (John 10:38).

"He that hath seen me hath seen the Father" (John 14:9).

"I am in the Father, and the Father in me" (John 14:10).

It is with the indirect evidence of this truth that I am dealing; and, as already noticed, the expert sets a high value upon evidence of that kind. Statements that teach explicitly the Deity of Christ may be frittered away by those who refuse the truth; but no one can thus evade the testimony supplied by the beliefs of the early disciples. And the force of that testimony is far greater than our theologians recognize. The learned treatises which discuss whether the Jew believed in a pre-existent *Divine* Messiah are strangely unintelligent. For, whether in the first century or the twentieth, it is only the spiritually enlightened who really believe in the Godhood of Christ; and every influence of the kind which, with us, leads men to give a blind assent to that doctrine, operated to prejudice the unregenerate Jew against it. The Gospels make it clear that with the little company of those who, in the midst of almost universal apostasy, were "waiting for the redemption," the question at issue was whether the Nazarene was really the Son of God; but with the ordinary Jew the very fact of His claiming to be Son of God was deemed conclusive evidence of blasphemy. The beliefs of the disciples, therefore, were formed and avowed in opposition to every influence which ecclesiastical authority could bring to bear on them.

In Christendom all who regard the Church as the oracle of God profess to believe Christ to be divine, just as they believe that the "consecrated wafer" is a symbol of His flesh. But the unregenerate Jew of nineteen hundred years ago stood intellectually on a higher level than the nominal Christian of today, for his beliefs rested upon Holy Scripture. And yet he shared the incapacity of all unspiritual men to receive its spiritual teaching. Indeed, the Sadducean heresies were merely a formal development of thoughts and doubts that are common to all unregenerate men whose minds are not warped or blinded by superstition. They prevail extensively today. For while the intellectual revolt of the sixteenth century re-established the authority of the Bible, and resulted in Protestantism, that of the seventeenth and eighteenth centuries led to an orgy of infidelity. And unfortunately the movement of our own day is not on the lines of the Reformation. But this is a digression.

Every Jew looked for a Messiah. But in Judaism there was no clear line of division between politics and religion; and so, while all expected him to be a prophet and a religious leader, the hopes of ordinary men were fixed on the coming of a great national champion who would deliver them from Gentile supremacy, and restore to them the prosperity and greatness of bygone days.[8]

But the faith of the little band of the Lord's disciples was far removed from the creeds and hopes of carnal men. "Thou art the Christ, the Son of the loving God" (Matt. 16:16); "Thou art the Son of God, thou art the King of Israel" (John 1:49): these were typical confessions. None but the Christ could be King of Israel, and Christ was the Son of God in the pregnant sense which that title signified. The confession of Thomas, "My Lord and my God" was the full expression of it. And if any one can suppose that devout Jews could have uttered such words to a fellow-creature, or that the Lord would have tolerated them had He not claimed to be divine, we have no common ground for a discussion of the question.

---

[8] A belief in *two* Messiahs, one to suffer, and one to reign in glory, seems to have been a popular solution of the difficulties which the study of the prophecies presented.

8

THE TESTIMONY OF PAUL

TO THE "beloved disciple" and the great Apostle of the Gentiles were entrusted the crowning revelations of the Christ.

The blindness of infidelity in rejecting on *a priori* grounds the verbal inspiration of Scripture is exposed even by the facts of Spiritualism—facts which are accredited by men of high character, some of whom are eminent as scientists and scholars. For these men testify to communications received from the spirit world; not mere impressions, nor yet trivial messages such as those of the days of "spirit-rapping," but serious verbal communications, sometimes spoken by human lips, sometimes written by the agency of a human hand.

To accept these facts and yet deny that the God who made us speak through inspired Prophets and Apostles, does not savor of intelligent skepticism, but of the folly of systematized unbelief.

But Spiritualism may also touch us more than most Christians seem to realize as to what inspiration means. The Apostle's words, "Forbidding to marry and commanding to abstain from meats" have reference to the Demon cult of these "latter times":[1] and so exacting is the fastidious asceticism of that cult that "mediums" are few. And we may be well assured that God requires an infinitely higher fitness in those through whom He will make revelations to His people. True it is that in extraordinary circumstances a

---

[1]The Christian knows that the spirits of spiritualistic seances are not the departed dead, but demons who personate them.

Sadducean priest may have been entrusted with a divine message to his fellows,[2] just as "a dumb ass" was once made use of to rebuke the madness of a prophet. But all the Hebrew seers, from Moses to Malachi, were trained for their ministry in the severest of divine schools. Like Him of whom they spoke, they were "made perfect through suffering."

And what was true of the prophets of the Old Testament was no less true of the holy men to whom the New Testament revelations were entrusted. For "I think," said the foremost of them, "God hath set forth us, the Apostles, last of all as men doomed to death: for we are made a spectacle unto the world, both to angels and to men. . . . We are made as the filth of the world and the offscouring of all things, even until now."[3] Here is his personal tale of suffering, even at a comparatively early stage of his ministry: "Of the Jews five times received I forty stripes save one. Thrice was I beaten with rods, once was I stoned, thrice I suffered shipwreck, a night and a day I have been in the deep; in journeyings often, in perils of waters, in perils of robbers, in perils by mine own countrymen, in perils by the heathen, in perils in the city, in perils in the wilderness, in perils in the sea, in perils among false brethren; in weariness and painfulness, in watchings often, in hunger and thirst, in fastings often, in cold and nakedness."[4]

"Once was I stoned." It is strange how little notice has been taken of the Apostle's martyrdom at Lystra. Stoning was a common death sentence under the Jewish law; and even when inflicted judicially the death was both swift and sure. But the stoning of Paul was not an execution, but a murder, and his murderers were men whose passions were inflamed by religious hate. The fierceness and brutality of

[2] John 11:49-51.
[3] I Corinthians 4:9-13.
[4] II Corinthians 11:24-27.

their action is indicated by the narrative. The ordinance which enjoined that stoning should be inflicted "outside the camp" was construed as requiring that, in the case of a city, it should take place outside the gate. But in their rage against Paul this was ignored; and so, after stoning him, "supposing that he was dead, they dragged him out of the city",[5] "dragged him," as they might have treated the carcass of a dog.

If the record ended there we might conjecture that the Apostle was borne away by the disciples, and lovingly nursed back to life, and that, after many weeks of suffering, he was able once again to resume his ministry. But among all the New Testament miracles of healing there is nothing more wonderful than what actually happened. For "as the disciples stood round about him *he rose up and entered into the city; and on the morrow he went forth with Barnabas to Derbe,*" and preached the gospel there. If ever there was a miracle, surely this was one!

Whether he had actually passed through the gates of death on that dreadful day, and been again called back to life, the Apostle never knew. But this he knew, that "whether in the body or out of the body"—whether dead or living— he had been "caught up even to the third heaven," and had heard unspeakable words. His vision on the Damascus road was again and again described by him, but the glory of Paradise and the words he heard there surpassed the possibilities of human utterance.

Well might he be "exalted overmuch" by "the exceeding greatness of the revelations"; and to humble him some trouble,

---

[5]Acts 14:19. "They stoned him, not in the Jewish method, but tumultuously and in the streets, dragging him out of the city afterwards" (Alford). "The full sense is 'And having prevailed on the multitude [to permit them to stone Paul], and having stoned him, they drew him out of the city.' *Suro* having reference to the brutal insults offered to the dead bodies of executed malefactors, which were usually dragged by the heels out of the city gates" (Bloomfield).

which he calls "a messenger of Satan," was permitted to make his life a martyrdom. The nature of that affliction has been the subject of many a conjecture. It evidently dated from the period of the "revelations";[6] and the inference is a natural one that it originated in the physical sufferings with which the "revelations" were associated. That it was something which tended to unfit him for his public ministry is evident—"something in his aspect or personality which distressed him with an agony of humiliation."[7]

One more clew is needed to guide us to a conclusion here. In Corinth his speech was deemed "contemptible," where as in his earlier ministry he had ranked as an orator. For though Barnabas was a man of no common capacity and mark, it was not Barnabas, but Paul, who was hailed at Lystra as "the god of eloquence." What, then, is the explanation of the seeming paradox? How natural that the stoning should have caused some facial paralysis, or some still more distressing affection which destroyed all control of his features, and made him an object of derision to the hostile or ill-conditioned members of every audience he addressed.[8] And this, I venture to suggest, was his "Gethsemane"—the affliction from which his thrice-repeated supplication sought

---

[6]"Evidently," I say, because the affliction was "given" to him lest the revelations should exalt him overmuch. The Romish exegesis of the passage, therefore, is certainly false. And the fact that Patristic authority can be cited for it does not deter me from describing it as shameful.

[7]Dean Farrar.

[8]It is very noteworthy that whenever he addressed cultured hearers, as, e.g., his various Roman judges, the Apostle seems to have commanded great consideration and respect. His affliction would draw out the courtesy of such men, while with the vulgar it might excite derision. And it is said that such an affliction would affect the sufferer in different degrees at different times.

deliverance.[9] The more we study that wonderful personality, the more unsatisfactory will seem the common view that it was a mere "thorn in the flesh"—some minor trouble of the kind that many a suffering Christian bears without a murmur. We may confidently follow those who understand his graphic words as meaning nothing less than "the agony of impalement."[10]

"Behold, I show you a mystery: We shall not all sleep, but *we shall all be changed*": with what a bounding heart the Apostle must have framed these words, as possibly he uttered them with twitching mouth, or penned them with shaking hand! And may we not in our little measure realize something of his calm, triumphant faith when, surveying his strangely tragic life, and recalling the vision of glory God had granted him, he wrote those further words, "I reckon that the sufferings of this present time are not worthy to be compared with the glory which shall be revealed to usward."[11]

Such are "the ways of God with men," or at least with those whom He singles out for special honor. And Paul

[9]II Corinthians 12. Bloomfield cites authorities for the conjecture that the trouble was "a paralytic and hypochondriac affection which occasioned a distortion of countenance and other distressing effects."

It has been urged upon me that this supposes an imperfect, an uncompleted, miracle of healing, for which there is no precedent in Scripture. But surely the Apostle's words indicate that he knew his experience to be peculiar. To suffer from "a thorn in the flesh" has been the lot of multitudes of the people of God, but to suffer impalement, as it were, from the after effects of injuries divinely healed—this was so unique that he twice refused to accept the answer to his prayer for relief.

[10]The word translated "thorn" means a stake for impaling, and then a thorn or splinter. Those who hold that ophthalmia was the Apostle's affliction appeal to Numbers 33:55 (LXX). The ablest statement known to me of that view is Dean Farrar's excursus in his "Life and Work of St. Paul." But the Apostle's references to his eyesight would all be accounted for if his trouble was of a kind that might be relieved by a present-day optician.

[11]Romans 8:18.

was chosen to be not merely the foremost witness of the risen Christ, but the recipient of the highest revelations concerning Him, revelations which reached a climax in the "Captivity Epistles."

Treatises have been written to prove that in turning to Jerusalem when the Lord had sent him to the Gentiles, he was a second Jonah, and that his imprisonment in Rome was a divine judgment. But this ignores the character of that Pentecostal dispensation in which the Jew had a priority in the offer of grace. And moreover, if it were true, surely some veiled reference to it would be found in his later Epistles. But there is none. "An ambassador in chains," and "the prisoner of the Lord"—such is his graphic description of his position in the imperial city; and this is not the language of a repentant Jonah.

May we not rather believe that all his steps were "ordered of the Lord"? And may it not be due to our crude and shallow estimate of what "inspiration" means, that we fail to realize that it was that very discipline that fitted him to receive and impart the crowning revelation of Christ? Nor should we forget that his ministry in writing the Epistles which contain that revelation was incomparably more important even than his evangelistic labors. Of the churches which he founded scarcely a trace survives, but those Epistles remain, the priceless and imperishable heritage of the people of God.

It is the intense and uncompromising monotheism of the Jew that gives such telling force to the incidental testimony which the Epistles supply to the Deity of Christ. And our knowledge of the personality and antecedents of the Apostle to the Gentiles lends immense weight to his words in this regard. A fanatical Pharisee in his unconverted days, and deeply versed in Rabbinical teaching, all his convictions and prejudices would have vetoed his using language which could be construed as an ascription of divine homage to any one but God. While, therefore, a phrase such as "Christ . . . who is over all, God blessed for ever," if written by one of the Greek Fathers, might possibly admit of the ingenious glosses of Socinian exegesis, its use by the Apostle is proof that with him the Godhood of Christ was a divine truth.[12]

The opening salutations of his Epistles, and also his "apostolic benediction," afford further proof of it, for in both the salutation and the benediction Christ is named as on the same level with God. "Grace to you, and peace from God our Father and the Lord Jesus Christ"; "The grace of our Lord Jesus Christ, and the love of God, and the communion of the Holy Ghost, be with you all." It is utterly inconceivable, I again repeat, that any man of Jewish training could have used such words unless the Lord Jesus Christ was enthroned in his heart as God.

And with an even greater force, if possible, does the remark apply to the Apostle's language in his later "captivity Epistles," written at the close of his life. Take, for example, his words to Titus: "Looking for the blessed hope and appearing of the glory of our great God and Saviour Jesus Christ; who gave himself for us that he might redeem us from all iniquity, and purify unto himself a people for his own possession."[13] This cannot be evaded by rejecting the revised reading of the words; for, however they are construed, the Lord Jesus is here named with God in a way

---

[12]I assume the correctness of the above rendering; and I am discussing the question without reference to inspiration. If the writings are inspired, there is no question left for discussion.

[13]Titus 2:13.

that to the Jewish mind would savor of blasphemy if He be not God.[14]

In this connection the charge to Timothy at the close of the first Epistle claims emphatic mention: "I charge thee in the sight of God . . . and of Christ Jesus . . . that thou keep the commandment, without spot, without reproach, until the appearing of our Lord Jesus Christ: which in its own times He shall shew, who is the blessed and only Potentate, the King of kings and Lord of lords; who only hath immortality, dwelling in light unapproachable; whom no man hath seen, nor can see: to whom be honour and power eternal. Amen."[15]

Commentators discuss the question, to which of the persons of the Trinity do these words refer? And those who apply the whole passage to "the Son" can urge that "the only Potentate" is equivalent to "our only Master and Lord" in Jude's Epistle, and that, in the Revelation, the title "King of kings and Lord of lords" is definitely given to Him whose "name is called the Word of God."[16] But I venture to suggest that it is because of the controversies on the subject that here, as in many another passage, we raise a question which may have had no place whatever in the mind of the Apostle.

[14]It is worthy of note that the identical words used of redemption by Jehovah in the Greek version of Exodus 19:5 are here quoted and applied to Christ. And also that the word "Saviour" occurs twice in each chapter of this Epistle, once of God and once of Christ. And though, of course, the word in itself does not connote Deity, it is incredible that the Apostle would have used it three times as a divine title, and three times in a lower sense when applied to Christ. The Christian will not doubt that it is used as a divine title in every one of its twenty-four occurrences in the New Testament, with the exception, perhaps, of Ephesians 5:23. And in fifteen of these occurrences it is used of Christ.

[15]I Timothy 6:13-16, R.V.

[16]Revelation 19:13, 16.

Not only in reading the Epistles, but even in their prayers, Christians often feel embarrassed by "the persons of the Trinity," for the meaning of that term is much misunderstood; but no trace of any such embarrassment can be found in Scripture. Indeed, paradoxical though it may seem, the difficulty we find in interpreting this sublime doxology and other kindred Scriptures is proof that no difficulty of the kind presented itself to the mind of the Apostle. For with him "the Son" was "our great God and Saviour." And in his words, therefore, there was no turning away from the Son to the Father; but by a natural transition his thoughts about "our Lord Jesus Christ" became merged in the thought of God.

I conclude by quoting a passage from each of the three principal Epistles written during his first imprisonment. The following is his prayer for the Ephesians:

"That the God of our Lord Jesus Christ, the Father of glory, may give unto you a spirit of wisdom and revelation in the knowledge of him; having the eyes of your heart enlightened that ye may know what is the hope of his calling, what the riches of the glory of his inheritance in the saints, and what the exceeding greatness of his power to usward who believe, according to that working of the strength of his might which he wrought in Christ, when he raised him from the dead, and made him to sit at his right hand in the heavenly places, far above all rule, and authority, and power, and dominion, and every name that is named, not only in this world, but also in that which is to come: and he put all things in subjection under his feet, and gave him to be head over all things to the church, which is his body, the fulness of him that filleth all in all" (Eph. 1:17-23).

To the Philippians he writes:

"Have this mind in you, which was also in Christ Jesus:

who, being in the form of God, counted it not a prize to
be on an equality with God, but emptied himself, taking
the form of a servant, being made in the likeness of men;
and being found in fashion as a man, he humbled himself,
becoming obedient even unto death, yea, the death of the
cross. Wherefore also God highly exalted him, and gave
unto him the name which is above every name; that in the
name of Jesus every knee should bow, of things in heaven,
and things on earth, and things under the earth, and that
every tongue should confess that Jesus Christ is Lord, to
the glory of God the Father" (Phil. 2:5-11).

And in the following passage from the Epistle to the
Colossians the revelation of Christ reaches its highest development:

"The Son of his love; in whom we have our redemption,
the forgiveness of our sins; who is the image of the invisible
God, the firstborn of all creation; for in him were all things
created, in the heavens and upon the earth, things visible
and things invisible, whether thrones, or dominions, or princi-
palities, or powers; all things have been created through him,
and unto him; and he is before all things, and in him all
things consist. And he is the head of the body, the church:
who is the beginning, the firstborn from the dead; that in
all things he might have the pre-eminence. For it was the
good pleasure of the Father that in him should all the
fulness dwell; and through him to reconcile all things unto
himself, having made peace through the blood of his cross;
through him, I say, whether things upon the earth, or things
in the heavens" (Col. 1:13-20).

To the unbeliever these words may seem the merest
rhapsody. But the Christian accepts them as Divine. And
to such I would appeal to read them again and again, and
to ponder them till mind and heart are saturated with them.
For I would say in the language of Ruskin—exaggerated

language when used with reference to human writings, but true and apt when applied to Holy Scripture—"You must get into the habit of looking intensely at words, and assuring yourself of their meaning, syllable by syllable—nay, letter by letter." And reading these Scriptures thus will dispel the last trace of unbelieving doubt as to who and what He is of whom they speak.

For no one who is not either mentally deficient or spiritually blind can imagine that such words refer to a fellow-creature.

9

THE TESTIMONY OF THE REVELATION

TO THE man of the world the Bible may seem to be
merely a chance collection of religious writings, but the
spiritual Christian finds abundant proof of its "hidden harmony" and organic unity. The book of Genesis is, as it
were, its opening chapter; and in the book of the Revelation
it reaches its legitimate conclusion. Genesis introduces us
to the *dramatis personæ* of the sacred volume, and gives us
an insight into its plot and purpose. There we have the
record of the Creation and the Fall, the judgment of the
Flood, the apostasy and scattering of the descendants of
Noah, the call of Abraham, and the origin of the chosen
people. And in the promise of "the seed of the woman,"
and in the typology of the book we have the prophecy and
pledge of Redemption.

And here in the Revelation all the dropped threads of
history and type and prophecy and promise, that lie scattered
throughout the earlier Scriptures, are taken up and traced
to their appointed consummation. Even in the opening
sections of the book the successive promises of "him that
overcometh" make cryptic reference to all the past. In
Ephesus the "overcomer" shares with unfallen Adam the
right to "the tree of life which is in the paradise of God."
In Smyrna he shares with Noah immunity from "the second
death"—the judgment which brought the first "dispensation"
to a close. In Pergamos he partakes with Moses of the
hidden manna; and in Thyatira he exercises kingly rule with
David. And Sardis speaks of the fellowship of the prophets,

and the reward for those who witness a good confession in days of apostasy.[1]

"The law and the prophets" were until John, whose mission it was to herald the coming of the Son of God. Then was ushered in a "dispensation" which, though brief as measured upon human calendars, was momentous beyond comparison—a transitional "dispensation" which, though Christian, was yet Jewish, and which ended with the destruction of all the externals of Judaism. In Philadelphia, therefore, the "overcomer" is called to share in the heavenly realities of which the temple that was the place of earthly worship, and the city which was the center of earthly blessing, were but shadows. In Laodicea, which represents the "dispensation" now drawing to a close, there is no reference to the past of Jewish symbolism or terminology; and the "overcomer" is a follower of Him who, as "the faithful and true Witness," has reached the throne by the path which led Him to the cross.[2]

All Scriptures is prophetic, because it is divine; but with special emphasis the Revelation is declared to be a prophecy. And as the main stream of prophecy always relates to Christ, the book fitly opens with a vision of His glory, and ends with a promise of His return. But by the majority of Christians both the vision and the promise are neglected or ignored. For His redeeming work is done and past, and therefore unspiritual men no longer need Him. And as the glory of His presence would put to shame the spiritual poverty and nakedness of those who profess to be His disciples, the thought of His return is embarrassing and unwelcome.

We are reminded of the Apostle's words, "Though we have known Christ after the flesh, yet now we know Him

[1]Revelation 2:7, 11, 17, 26, 27; 3:5.
[2]Revelation 3:12, 21, 22.

so no longer."[3] Not that the Christian gives up one jot or tittle of the record of the Saviour's earthly life, but that his faith rests upon his risen and glorified and coming Lord, and he reaches back from the Christ of the glory to the Christ of the humiliation. But "the Christian religion" is founded upon "Christ after the flesh"; and this influence governs the thoughts and the language even of spiritual Christians. Its deplorable effect upon our religious literature is apparent everywhere. Too many of our standard theological treatises, indeed, and of our popular "books of piety," would seem almost unchristian if read in the light of the visions of glory vouchsafed to the Apostle John, or of the great doctrinal revelations entrusted to the Apostle Paul. And as these Scriptures would thus disturb habits of thought and speech "received by tradition from our fathers," we ignore them, and cling to our "Christ after the flesh" religion.

One result is that the old "Evangelicalism" gives way before the inroads of Rationalism and superstition. Under the pressure of aggressive skepticism many find rest by taking a deeper plunge into a false religion. Orthodoxy may thus be maintained by blindly obeying "the voice of the Church"; but orthodoxy is not faith, nor is the voice of the Church the Word of God. With the young, however, the lapse is usually toward "modernism," and the skeptical movement which masquerades as "the Higher Criticism."

The men who—in this country at least—champion that crusade are not chargeable with intentional disloyalty to Christ, for they fail to understand its true character and ultimate aim. The imagery of the last chapter of Ephesians is borrowed from the battlefield; and one way in which military genius shows itself is in a capacity to detect the real objective of an enemy's advance. The attack on Holy

[3]II Corinthians 5:16.

Scripture is but a feint, and these men are blindly fulfilling their part in a strategic movement which is directed against Christ. For it is only through the written Word that we can reach the Living Word; and if we give up the one, we lose both.

But, it is said, how can the rejection of such a book as Daniel, for instance, affect our faith in Christ? If Daniel be jettisoned, the Revelation goes overboard along with it, and a signally important testimony to the Deity of Christ is lost to us. But more than this, if "Moses and the prophets" be discredited, we are confronted by the fact that the Lord identified Himself with their writings; and we are forced to conclude, either that the records of His teaching are unreliable, or else that He was Himself the dupe of false and superstitious beliefs. If the one alternative be accepted, the "rock of Holy Scripture" proves to be a quicksand. Or if, as the critics boast, the other alternative is "an assured result" of the new enlightenment, no one who is not hypnotized by superstition will cling to the dogma of His Deity. Such passages as the first chapter of Colossians must be dismissed as the rhapsody of an enthusiast, and the visions of the Apocalypse as the day-dreams of a brilliant mystic.

But the theme of these pages is not the divine authority of Scripture, but the Deity of Christ; and what specially concerns us here is the testimony to that truth which the Apocalypse affords.

In the preface to the book the whole is described as "the prophecy"; and while some expositors would exclude the Epistles to the Churches from that category, it is universally admitted that all which follows falls within it. And no careful reader can fail to see that if "the Lamb" of these visions be not God, He has everywhere supplanted God. From the fourth chapter to the end "the Father" is never named but once; and then it is not in contrast with "the Lamb," but in closest union with Him. It occurs in the vision of the fourteenth chapter, where the Seer beholds the Lamb standing on Mount Sion, "and with Him a hundred and forty-four thousand, having *His name and His Father's name* written in their foreheads."[4]

And so also in the later visions. Chapter 19 opens with the heavenly anthem, "Hallelujah, salvation, and glory, and honour, and power unto the Lord our God; for true and righteous are his judgments." It is the doom of the apostate church on earth that evokes this burst of praise in heaven. And then, in response to a voice from the throne, the further anthem rises "as the voice of mighty thunders," "Hallelujah; for the Lord God Omnipotent reigneth." And, from an opened heaven there comes forth One whom now we know as the Saviour, but who is here revealed as the Avenger. "His eyes are a flame of fire, and upon His head are many diadems. . . . And He is arrayed in a garment sprinkled with blood, and His name is called the Word of God." It is not "the blood of sprinkling that speaketh better things than that of Abel," but the blood of Isaiah's prophecy of vengeance.[5] For now Isaiah's words are about to be fulfilled: "The day of vengeance is in mine heart, and the year of my redeemed is come."

And the Seer adds: "He hath on His garment and on His thigh a name written, King of kings and Lord of lords." This is the public title of Him whose mystery name is "the Word of God." His identity is thus made clear. And let us keep steadily in view that the God of the Bible is One; and that He is manifested in Christ, and revealed by the Holy Spirit.

More plainly still does this appear in the final vision of the heavenly City. There is no temple in the New Jerusalem,

[4]Revelation 14:1, R.V.
[5]Isaiah 63.

for "the Lord God Almighty and the Lamb are the temple thereof." No need for sun or moon to shine on it, "for the glory of God did lighten it, and the Lamb is the light thereof." "And the throne of God and of the Lamb shall be in it; and His servants shall serve Him, and they shall see His face, and His name shall be in their foreheads."

One throne, one temple, one light—God and the Lamb, inseparably One. So absolute the unity that "laws of thought" and "rules of grammar" are ignored; and though God *and* the Lamb are the burden of the vision, it is His name the redeemed are said to bear, and His face it is that they shall see.

To drag these visions down to the level of religious controversy would be deplorable. Let us ponder them until our minds are saturated with the very words in which they are revealed, and all doubt will be dispelled as to the God-hood of the Christ who died for us. Or if the shadow of a doubt still lingers, the sequel may suffice to banish it. For when the Apostle prostrates himself in worship at the feet of the glorious being who has been his guide and teacher in these heavenly visions, he is peremptorily checked. "See thou do it not," the angel exclaims; "I am a fellow-servant with thee and with thy brethren the prophets, and with them that keep the words of this book: worship God." The highest of created beings is a fellow-servant with the humblest saint. And if Christ be not God, even He must stand on this same level, and all worship rendered to Him is idolatrous and sinful.

And now, with this inexorable alternative in view, we turn again to the opening chapter. "The revelation of Jesus Christ" is the divinely given title of the book, and it governs the whole contents of it. In this light, then, we read the words, "I am the Alpha and the Omega, saith the Lord God, who is, and who was, and who is to come, the Almighty." Certain it is that "the Alpha and the Omega" is a title which belongs to God alone; and if any should doubt whether it here refers to the Lord Jesus, the fact remains that it is claimed by Him expressly in the concluding message of the book: "I am the Alpha and the Omega, the first and the last, the beginning and the end. . . . I, Jesus, have sent Mine angel to testify these things unto you for the Churches." That same voice it was that summoned the Seer to behold the opening vision of the book. Here is the record of it:

"I saw seven golden candlesticks, and in the midst of the seven candlesticks one like unto the Son of Man, clothed with a garment down to the foot, and girt about the paps with a golden girdle. His head and his hairs were white like wool, as white as snow; and his eyes were as a flame of fire; and his feet like unto fine brass, as if they burned in a furnace; and his voice as the sound of many waters. And he had in his right hand seven stars; and out of his mouth went a sharp two-edged sword: and his countenance was as the sun shineth in his strength. And when I saw him, I fell at his feet as dead. And he laid his right hand upon me, saying unto me, Fear not; I am the first and the last: I am he that liveth and was dead; and, behold, I am alive for evermore, and I have the keys of hell and of death."[6]

"The simple and natural conclusion is that Jesus was the child of Joseph and Mary, and had an uneventful childhood."

Such is the alternative belief which the infidel offers us in exchange for the faith of Christ. And my apology for quoting words which cannot fail to outrage Christian feeling is that, in these days of levity and superficial thought, many who would resent a charge of apostasy are in danger of drifting away from the faith of Christ; and therefore it is well to make them realize the peril which threatens them.

---

[6]Revelation 1:12-18.

For to deny the Deity of the Lord Jesus Christ is to bring Him down to the level of mere humanity; and the foundations of Christianity being thus destroyed, the whole superstructure falls to pieces. The doctrine of an atoning death is gone. "Indeed the very suggestion is absurd," the writer above quoted tells us. And Gethsemane and Calvary will thus find many a parallel, not only in the story of the martyrs, but in the sufferings of common men. For, he adds, "many a British soldier has died as brave a death as Jesus"; and "an immense amount of pious nonsense has been spoken and written about our Lord's agony in Gethsemane. . . . Your agony would be just as great as that of Jesus."

The natural refinement and courtesy of writers such as the distinguished Rationalist quoted on the opening page of this volume lead them to conceal the legitimate deductions from their misbelief, lest the statement of them should shock or wound Christian sentiment. But the writer above quoted is unrestrained by any considerations of the kind. And his words may do good if, just by reason of their wanton profanity and coarseness, they lead the trifler and the waverer to realize the nature of the abyss to which apostasy from Christ will lead them.

10

FOR HIS NAME'S SAKE

NO ONE who accepts the Scriptures as divine is entitled to deny that in His personal ministry the Lord Jesus laid claim to Deity. And the crucifixion is a public proof that He did in fact assert this claim. For we are told expressly that the reason why the Jews plotted His death was "because he not only brake the Sabbath but also called God his own Father, making himself equal with God."[1] His claim to be "Lord even of the Sabbath" was in itself an assertion of equality with the God of Sinai. And as regards His declaring Himself to be the Son of God, the question is not what these words might convey to English readers today, but what He Himself intended His hearers to understand by them.[2]

And this He made unequivocally clear. The charge brought against Him was one from which, if false, any godly Israelite would have recoiled with horror. But instead of repelling it He accepted it in a way which even common men could understand. For He immediately asserted such absolute unity with God that the Father was responsible for His every act, including, of course, the miracle which they had denounced as a violation of the divine law. He next claimed absolute equality with God as "the author and giver of life"—the supreme prerogative of Deity. And, lastly, He asserted His exclusive right to the equally divine prerogative of judgment.[3]

---

[1]John 5:18.
[2]See chapter IV.
[3]See verses 19-22 of John 5.

My object in recapitulating this now and here is to seize upon the words which follow, for they are words which may well cause searching of heart to the Christian in these days of ours. The reason why all judgment has been committed to Him is, He declared, "in order that all may honour the Son *even as they honour the Father*."[4] And to make this still more emphatic He added, "He that honoureth not the Son, honoureth not the Father which sent him."

Men of the world think of Him only as the great Buddha who once lived and died on earth. They know nothing of the living Lord who now reigns in Heaven. It seems natural to them, therefore, to speak of Him as "a man by the name of Jesus Christ," or, with still more distressing freedom, as simply "Jesus." But how is it that real Christians, who profess to honor Him "even as they honour the Father," habitually offend in the same way? It is to be hoped that with very many the fault is due to mere thoughtlessness or ignorance; and if these pages should lead any such to clear themselves from this reproach, they will not have been written in vain.

"Sanctify Christ in your hearts *as Lord*" is an exhortation we need to remember. And if He be enshrined in the heart as Lord, the confession of the lip will be a matter of course. This confession, indeed, is at once a characteristic and a proof of discipleship; for "no one can say, 'Lord Jesus' but by the Holy Spirit."[5] Any lips, of course, could frame the words; but it is a fact of extraordinary interest that the unspiritual never do say, "Lord Jesus." They may call Him

---

[4]John 5:23. In English this might mean no more than honoring the Son in addition to honoring the Father. But the words used by the Lord imply rendering to the Son the same honor as is rendered to the Father. He uses the word eight times in chap. 17. (verses 2, 11, 14, 16, 18, 21, 22, 23) and it always implies "even as," "in the same way as."

[5]I Corinthians 12:3.

"Jesus," or "Jesus Christ," or use some such term as "our Saviour"; but "the Lord Jesus"—never!

In New Testament times the disciple thus declared himself by the way in which he named his Lord.[6] It was not that he followed a set rule, but that he obeyed a spiritual instinct. And so it ought to be with us. In the social sphere it is not by rule, but by an instinct of courtesy, that we address other people, and speak of them, in a becoming manner; and in this sphere our spiritual instincts would be a still more unerring guide if they were not deadened and depraved by the baneful influences which prevail around us.

It is recorded in the Acts that "certain of the strolling Jews, exorcists, took upon them to name over them that had evil spirits the name of the Lord Jesus, saying, I adjure thee by Jesus, whom Paul preacheth." Mark the words. To the disciples He was "the Lord Jesus," but to the vagabond Jews He was "Jesus." And Christendom follows the example, not of the disciples, but of the vagabond Jews!

But it is said, "Why should we not call Him 'Jesus'? Is He not thus named hundreds of times in the Gospels?" Strange it is that people who contend vehemently for the inspiration of Scripture should thus give proof that they have no faith in it. For if it means anything, it implies a divine authorship of the sacred books, controlling the authorship of the human writers.

If "The Letters of Queen Victoria" had been published anonymously, the mode in which they name the members of the Royal Family would in itself indicate the queen as writer. And the manner in which the "Son of His love" is named in the evangelistic records is one of the many incidental proofs that the Gospels are indeed "the Word of God." What makes

---

[6]This appears both from the Gospel narrative and from the Lord's express commendation of the practice: "Ye call me Master and Lord, and *ye say well*" (John 13:13).

this so especially significant is the fact that while in the main narrative the Lord is always "Jesus," yet *in every instance* where the narrative introduces words spoken by the disciples as such, whether addressed to Him or to others about Him, a title of reverence is used.

The case of the disciples with whom He went to Emmaus on the day of the resurrection may seem to be an exception, but it is a most significant one. They had hoped that "it was He who should redeem Israel," but their hope had been shattered by the crucifixion. And now that He was dead, He was no longer "the Lord," but merely "Jesus of Nazareth."[7]

It is idle to discuss this with any who seek excuses for refusing to render to Him the homage which He claims from His people. But the devout will recognize that in this matter they should be guided by the Lord's own teaching, and by the example of those who received the teaching from His own lips. And here we are not left in doubt. His words, "Ye call me 'Master' and 'Lord,' and ye say well," give proof of their invariable practice, and of His unqualified approval of it; and surely this should be enough for us.

In this matter the testimony of the Epistles is of extraordinary interest. For while in the Gospels the Lord is named narratively as "Jesus" some six hundred times,[8] the simple name occurs only twenty-two times in the whole range of the Epistles. And it never once occurs by way of narrative mention: there is always a special reason for its use.

---

[7]Luke 24:19. During His life the Jews called Him "Jesus of Nazareth" merely as a distinctive name, and thus it was that Cleopas used it. But after His death it became a name of reproach—the name of the false Messiah who had been crucified as a blasphemer. And it is with this signification, as equivalent to "the despised and rejected of men," that it was used by the Apostles in Acts 2:22, 10:38, and 26:9, and by the Lord Himself to Paul (Acts 22:8).

[8]The disciples never call Him "Jesus," whereas the main narrative always names Him thus.

If the relative dates of the New Testament books were different, a plausible explanation of this might be attempted. But in view of the facts it must be an insoluble enigma to those who deny the inspiration of the Scriptures.

An illustrative instance will explain what is meant by the narrative use of the Lord's human name. The Evangelists record that at the Last Supper "Jesus took bread"; but in the Epistle to the Corinthians we read "The Lord Jesus took bread." In all the Apostle Paul's Epistles, indeed, there are only eight passages in which the Lord is named as "Jesus"; and in each of these there is either a special emphasis or a doctrinal significance in the use of the name of His humiliation.[9]

This appears in a very striking way in the only two passages in which "the simple name" occurs in all his six later Epistles, written in his Roman prisons. In Ephesians the Apostle writes: "Ye did not so learn Christ; if so be that ye heard Him and were taught in Him, even as truth is in Jesus." Here the "Jesus" is emphatic; for the exhortation relates to the practical life of the Christian, which ought to be governed by the teaching of Christ as the truth was manifested in the example of His own life on earth in the time of His humiliation.[10]

And in writing to the Philippians, he presents in striking contrast the Lord's humiliation on earth and His exaltation to the place of supreme glory and power in heaven. And it was because He humbled Himself that God exalted Him

---

[9]"The use of the simple name 'Jesus' is rare in the Epistles." "Wherever it occurs it will be found to be distinctive or emphatic." "The modern familiar use of the simple name 'Jesus' has little authority in Apostolic usage" (Bishop Ellicott's "New Testament Commentary for English Readers": Ephesians 4:21.)

[10]Ephesians 4:21 (II Corinthians 4:10 is a similar passage). A misreading of this verse has given rise to the popular phrase, "the truth as it is in Jesus," meaning thereby evangelical doctrine. In scriptural language that would be called "the truth of *Christ*." And it is not doctrine, but practice, that is here indicated.

thus, and "gave Him the name that is above every name." Surely we cannot err in connecting this with His glory as exalted "above every name that is named, not only in this world, but also in that which is to come." What can that name be but the great name of Jehovah?

But it is "in the name of Jesus" that every knee shall bow. What can this mean but that it is as the man of Nazareth and Calvary that He will command the worship of every being in the universe, while all shall unite to own that He is Lord?

The name of His humiliation is thus placed in marked antithesis to that of His glory; and the passage should teach us, not to call Him "Jesus," but to confess that He is Lord.[11]

When reading these Epistles which were definitely addressed to *Hebrew* Christians, it is specially important to keep in mind the place which the Messianic title held with the Jew. If in I Peter, for instance, we read "Messiah," or "the Christ," in every place where "Christ" is used, and "Jesus the Messiah" wherever "Jesus Christ" occurs, the unfamiliar terms will, in some measure, bring to our minds what the words conveyed to Jewish ears. For I would take sides with those who refuse to believe that "Christ" is ever used merely as a proper name. With the Jew it was a sacred title of great solemnity; and it is hard to believe that a Hebrew Christian could have come to regard it in any other light.[12]

---

[11]The passages here cited are given earlier in this chapter. I would urge that, as the name of His glory is conferred on Him *because He humbled Himself*, it cannot be the name of His humiliation. And if the Apostle meant thereby the name of "Jehovah," he used the only word which the Greek language supplied to express it. Alford's exegesis amounts to this, that because He humbled Himself to become Jesus, God gave Him *that same name* with a new dignity attached to it. This seems to me to fritter away the meaning of the passage, and to ignore the force of verse 10. I need not say that bowing *at* the name is not its teaching.

[12]The assumption, indeed, exemplifies the want of appreciation of Jewish thought and feeling that is so characteristic of "Gentile" exegesis.

The Epistles of Peter give striking proof that the terminology of the Epistles in this respect was influenced by the proclivities of those to whom they were addressed. In his first Epistle for example, which was written expressly for Israelites, the Lord is named twelve times as "Christ,"[13] and eight times as "Jesus Christ"; for with the Israelite the Messianic title would carry its own solemn and sacred significance. But to Gentiles "Christ" might seem to be a proper name, and "Jesus Christ" merely a double name (like Simon Peter); and therefore, in his second Epistle, which was not addressed exclusively to Hebrews, he never once names Him by the simple title of "Christ," and only once as "Jesus Christ." In his opening salutation he describes himself as "the bondservant of Jesus Christ"—it seems to have been a regular apostolic formula—but in the very same sentence he goes on to designate Him as "our God and Saviour Jesus Christ," and again as "Jesus our Lord." Three times we have "our Lord Jesus Christ,"[14] and three times "our Lord and Saviour Jesus Christ."[15]

If these words were merely of a converted Jew they would be overwhelming proof of a belief in the Deity of Christ. For it is indeed "Gentile ignorance" to suppose that a devout Jew could use such language of any created being, however exalted. But they are the words of an inspired Apostle; and to reject such testimony is to undermine the authority of Holy Scripture.

Upon the main subject of this chapter I would make a parting appeal. Tendencies are just now declaring themselves in political and social life, which cause forebodings in the minds of thoughtful men. But these are of little moment

---

[13]Following the Revised text, I include I Peter 5:10 and 14, where the A.V. reads "Christ Jesus"; and 3:15, where it reads "Lord God."
[14]II Peter 1:8, 14 and 16.
[15]II Peter 1:11; 2:20; and 3:18.

in comparison with the development of evils, as subtle as they are grave, in the religious sphere. The lists seem to be preparing for the great predicted struggle of the latter days between the apostasy of avowed infidelity and the apostasy which flaunts the name of Christ upon its banners. The one pays homage to "the historic Jesus," who is *primus inter pares,* the best and greatest of mankind. The other worships a mythical "Jesus" who takes rank with a mythical "mother of God." Both alike are opposed to Christ. For the truth that He is "God over all, blessed for ever," which the one openly rejects, the other implicitly undermines. And these evils seem to be daily gathering volume and force. Their influence is clearly manifest in our religious literature; and it is more and more corrupting the faith of Christians of every class and school.

It would seem to me, therefore, that even if we could find a scriptural warrant—*and I can find none*—for liberty to name the Lord of Glory with the easy familiarity so common in these evil days, we should do well to forego that liberty, and to give proof by our very words, in season and out of season, that we are of the number of those who own Him as Lord, and who honor Him "even as they honor the Father." The confession of Him thus as Lord is the very essence of the gospel. "For if thou shalt confess with thy mouth Jesus *as Lord,* and shalt believe in thine heart that God raised Him from the dead, thou shalt be saved."[16]

But "the god of this world hath blinded the minds of the unbelieving, that the light of the gospel of the glory of Christ, who is the image of God, should not dawn upon them."[17]

The gospel of a "Jesus" who is the image of man is his chief device to delude his votaries today. But "we preach

[16]Romans 10:9, R.V.   [17]II Corinthians 4:4, R.V.

Christ Jesus as Lord," the Apostle immediately adds; and this the devil cannot tolerate, for it impugns "the lie" of which he is the father—the lie that he himself is the true "firstborn," to whom the sovereignty of the world by right belongs.[18]

---

[18]I make bold to read John 8:44 literally. "When he speaks *the* lie, he speaks of his own; for he is a liar, and the father of it." And so also in II Thessalonians 2:11. For "the lie," see Luke 4:5, 6.

11

GRACE AND THE LIFE TO COME

"THE SON of God is come!" The Eden promise of the
woman's seed was like the little rivulet far up a mountain side,
to which men point as the beginning of a mighty river. Down
through the centuries type was added to type, and prophecy
to prophecy, enlarging its scope and unfolding its meaning,
until the completed Hebrew Scriptures became a deep, broad
stream of hope and promise. And when the fulness of the
time had come, "God sent His only begotten Son into the
world," and promise and hope became merged in glorious
fact.

The primeval revelation was enshrined in the traditions
of the human race, and took shape in many fantastic forms
in the mythologies of the ancient world. But nothing in the
wildest fancies of pagan religions or of classic poetry is so
utterly incredible to the natural mind as is the truth of Christ.
"The gods are come down to us in the likeness of men," was
a cry that excited but little either of skepticism or of wonder;
for, having regard to the character of their gods, such a descent
was natural and easy. But that God, who is spirit, has been
"manifested in flesh"; that God, whom the heaven of heavens
cannot contain, has revealed Himself on earth, and revealed
Himself "in the likeness of men";[1] that the Man of Nazareth,
"the son of the carpenter," the crucified Jew, was the Word
who was in the beginning with God, and was Himself God,
the Creator of all things that exist, and apart from whom

[1]Mark the kinship of the words of the pagan idolaters in Acts 14:11,
and of the inspired Apostle in Philippians 2:7.

nothing that exists came into being—this seems to be outside the limits, not only of what is possible in fact, but of what is conceivable in human imagination. Hence the deep meaning of the words with which the Lord received the Apostle Peter's confession of His Deity: "Blessed art thou, Simon Bar-Jonah; for flesh and blood hath not revealed it unto thee, but My Father which is in heaven." Can we wonder at His declaring that "no one knoweth the Son save the Father"!

We think of the Nazarene as He taught by the Lake of Galilee, or in the Temple courts, surrounded by peasants and fishermen, but shunned by all people of culture or repute not only in the social, but in the religious sphere; and we remember that the last the world ever saw of Him was hanging on a gibbet between two common criminals. And as we ponder these things we begin to appreciate the meaning of the challenge, "Who is he that overcometh the world, but he that believeth that Jesus is the Son of God!" *Jesus*, "the despised and rejected of men," the outcast heretic, the crucified blasphemer—that He is the Son of God! The faith that thus takes sides with God against the world is a faith that overcomes the world, "For whosoever believeth that *Jesus* is the Christ is born of God." Hence it is that God is "the justifier of him that hath faith in *Jesus*"; for "as many as received *him*, to them gave he the right to become children of God." (I John 1:9).

With the mass of men who profess the Christian creed, what passes for faith is but a surface current on the smooth and shallow stream of their religious impressions. Most of us "believe" that the earth is a sphere, and that it is twirling on its axis and spinning round the sun. This venerable hypothesis is scientifically useful, and, moreover, it is probably true. But if "science" should discover tomorrow that it is false, the discovery would not spoil our appetite for a single meal, or rob us of our sleep for a single night. And there

are multitudes of professing Christians who in recent years
have bartered their conventional faith in Christ for the coarse
profanity of the "New Theology," or the pleasing and plausible
fallacies and falsehoods of "Christian Science"; and the
change has served only to increase their self-esteem and their
enjoyment of existence.

A mere creed orthodoxy has but little in common with
true faith in Christ. And yet the many organized phases of
latter-day apostasy could not work such havoc among professing Christians, were it not that orthodoxy is paralyzed
by the crusade of recent years against the divine authority
of Scripture. In the physical sphere, when life loses its
aggressive power, and can no longer overcome the forces
that produce decay, vital energy soon fails; and so it is
here. Evangelicalism, attacked on one side by superstition
and on the other by rationalism, has been content to stand
upon the defensive, and to sacrifice truth for the sake of
peace and so-called unity. The enthusiasm of faith has been
killed by the spirit of compromise.

Plain speaking is needed in times like these. "To him
that overcometh" is the prevailing note in the Lord's last
messages of warning and cheer to His people upon earth.
For when churches fail, He counts upon individual faith-
fulness. And in these days of ours organized Christianity
has failed, and the defense of the truth has become "a
soldier's battle." In too many of our pulpits, indeed, the
commonly received "doctrines of the Christian religion"—
man's sin and ruin, redemption by blood, the resurrection of
the dead, and eternal judgment—are openly assailed or
implicitly denied. And from most of our pulpits the distinctive
truths of Christianity are never heard. For doctrines such
as those above enumerated are not distinctively Christian at
all. As the Epistle to the Hebrews tells us, they are a part
of the divine revelation of Judaism. They are "the first

principles of the oracles of God," or, in other words, the
elements of revealed religion.

But the Christian revelation is a revelation about Christ.
Not that "a man of the name of Jesus Christ once stood in
our midst," that He worked great miracles, taught great
truths, lived a holy life, and died a shameful death—all this
a wayfaring man, though a fool, can discover for himself
by human testimony; but that the man who thus lived and
died on earth was the Son of God (and we have seen what
that title signifies—"the Lord of Glory," "our great God and
Saviour"); and that He is now sitting on the throne of God,
in all the glory of God, and with all power in heaven and on
earth. In view of all this—seemingly so incredible, and yet so
divinely true—we can understand His words, "When the
Son of Man cometh, shall He find the faith upon the earth?"

Though in the natural sphere we can put pressure on the
sane and the intelligent to acknowledge facts and to yield to
reason, we cannot compel belief in Christ, for spiritual truth
is spiritually discerned. And yet we may be able to clear
away mists of ignorance and barriers of error, that prejudice
and blind the minds of men. The Christian revelation is
apparently falsified by facts. If the Christ of the Ministry be
indeed Almighty God, wielding all power on earth, what explanation can be offered of this world's evil and hateful history
throughout the Christian era? "The times of the restoration
of all things," or, in other words, the times when everything
should be put right on earth, were the burden of Hebrew
prophecy. But the hope was to be realized at the advent of
Messiah; and yet, after nineteen centuries, it seemingly remains but a dream of poets and mystics.

Platitudes about the goodness and wisdom of an inscrutable
Providence will neither silence the infidel nor satisfy His suffering people. But the Lord's words last quoted were spoken
in connection with other words which point to the solution

of the mystery. God will indeed avenge His own elect, though He is *longsuffering* respecting them. Or, as the Apostle Peter wrote, recalling, doubtless, these very words, "the Lord is not slack concerning his promise as some count slackness, but is *longsuffering.*"[2]

The great truth of grace was lost between the days of the Apostles and the age of the Patristic theologians. As the sun breaks forth on a typical April day, and then again becomes veiled in clouds, this truth flashed out in the teaching of the Reformation, and then disappeared again. Though Luther was its foremost champion, the Church which bears his name systematically denies it; and it is practically ignored by the great theological schools of Calvin and Arminius. And yet it is the truth which alone will teach us to "justify the ways of God with men."

He to whom all judgment is committed, and who wields all power, is exalted to be a *Saviour,* and His reign is a reign of *Grace.* When in the synagogue of Nazareth He stood up to read the appointed lesson from the prophets, He closed the book at the middle of its opening sentence. "To preach the acceptable year of the Lord" were the last words He uttered. And as all eyes were fastened on Him—well might they stare in wonder—"He began to say unto them, This day is this Scripture fulfilled in your ears." "*And the day of vengeance of our God*" were the words before Him on the page, but He left these words unread.

And by reason of the longsuffering of God the dawning of that awful day is still deferred. It is not that the moral government of the world is in abeyance, but that divine *judicial* action is postponed until the day of grace shall have run its course. And this of necessity. For if all judgment is committed to the Lord Jesus Christ—all judicial and punitive action re-

[2]Luke 18:7; II Peter 3:9. It is the same word in both passages.

specting sin—the day of grace must run its course before the judgment can begin. The great amnesty has been proclaimed—forgiveness and peace for sinful men; and while this ministry of reconciliation lasts, judgment there cannot be. The functions of Saviour and Judge are incompatible. He must relinquish the throne of grace before He takes His place on the throne of judgment.

"All power is of God," but the power of rule on earth is now delegated to men, and men are incompetent and corrupt. But the day is coming when "the mystery of God shall be finished," and the rule of this world shall become our Lord's and His Christ's. Then shall be heard the anthem, "We give Thee thanks, O Lord God Almighty, because Thou hast taken to Thee Thy great power and hast reigned, and Thy wrath has come." And then shall He give reward to His people and destroy them who destroy the earth.[3]

A pandemonium ended by a bonfire might epigrammatically describe the divine government of the world, as travestied by our popular theology. But in the light of Scripture all is clear and plain. True it is that this earth that has been the scene of the pandemonium, shall yet be given up to fire, but not till every word of Hebrew prophecy has been fulfilled; for no word can fail that God has ever uttered. "We according to His promise, look for new heavens and a new earth," but this belongs to an eternity to come. It is *in time* as measured upon human calendars, and here on this earth of ours, now blighted by human sin, that divine goodness and power shall yet be displayed in righteous rule.

Of the fulfilment of this hope "God hath spoken by all his holy prophets since the world began,"[4] and "the mystery of God" is that its fulfilment is delayed. And yet by the mass of those who profess to believe the Scriptures it is treated as

[3]Revelation 10:7; 11:15-18.
[4]Acts 3:21.

a dream of visionaries, and not a few there are who scoff at it. Though they pray "Thy kingdom come, Thy will be done on earth," they refuse to tolerate the thought that the Lord will fufil the prayer which He Himself has given us. In the religious sphere, indeed, it would seem that men will believe anything except the truth of God, and thousands of our pulpits promote the delusion that the work of the churches will yet result in the conversion of the world.

Were the subject not so solemn, ridicule would be our fittest weapon against a figment so grotesque. In the days of the Ministry the "professing church" on earth had been so thoroughly absorbed by the world that it was itself "the world" against which the Lord so strenuously warned His disciples. And in our day "the church" is not converting the world, but becoming assimilated to the world. Man is God's creature, and therefore by nature a religious being. But he is a fallen creature, and therefore his religion always tends downwards. And the god of this world caters for the idiosyncrasies of his dupes. For one the lure is the elevation of humanity, for another, it is to bring the Deity down to his own level: rationalism and superstition—the cult of the Eden lie,[5] and the cult of the golden calf[6]—these are now the evangels of the Churches of the Reformation; and the men who keep to the old gospel are a dwindling minority.

But the last note struck in these concluding pages shall not be controversy, but appeal and hope. "O fools, and slow of heart to believe all that the prophets have spoken," was the Lord's rebuke to His disciples because their faith had given way under a strain such as none had ever known before, and

---

[5]"Your eyes shall be opened, and ye shall be as gods" (Gen. 3:5).

[6]Exodus 32:1-6. The calf was the victim in the great burnt-offering of the covenant (Exodus 24); and the idol was an outward symbol to represent the spiritual reality. It was worshipped at "a feast to the Lord" (verse 5) only in the sense in which altars and crosses are now worshipped.

none could ever know again. He whom they had worshipped as Messiah had been crucified in shame; and was not His corpse lying in the tomb![7] Yet fools they were to doubt, even in face of facts so stern and so terrible, that the words of the prophets were divine, or to think that God could fail to fulfill them to the last jot and tittle. And we may well give heed to that rebuke, and take it to ourselves—we whose faith breaks down because, forsooth, in the longsuffering of God, with whom a thousand years are as one day, the fulfilment of the promise is delayed![8]

When toward the close of His ministry the Lord warned His people of times of trouble, which may now perhaps be near at hand, He spoke words well fitted to create feelings of despair. But His purpose was far different, for immediately He added, "When these things begin to come to pass, then look up, and lift up your heads, for your redemption draweth nigh."[9] "Look up," for our hope is in His coming. "The second advent" of our theology belongs to a future too remote to influence our lives; and, moreover, it is associated only with the thought of judgment. But His coming was the hope of His people in a bygone age, and it is the true hope of His people still. Upon His coming, indeed, depends their full redemption; for we have bodies as well as souls, and our bodies are still subject to that hideous outrage, death. For death is none the less an enemy because He has triumphed over it, and has given the victory to us.

And beyond the hope of His believing people—that true church which He Himself is building—there lies the hope of Israel, yet to be restored to favor when the "professing

---

[7]Luke 24:21, 25.
[8]In his famous Birmingham address on "Science and Man," Prof. Tyndall said, "The promise is a dream marred by the experience of eighteen centuries." And Christians here take sides with the skeptic!
[9]Luke 21:28.

church" of this "Christian" age of ours shall have received its doom.[10] And beyond the hope of Israel there lies the hope of this sin-blighted world, for the sovereignty of the world is to become His;[11] and "even the creation itself shall be delivered from the bondage of corruption."[12] And as our faith dwells upon this glorious vista of prophecy and promise yet to be fulfilled, let us remember that all is for the glory of Him whom we know as our Lord and Saviour, and (it cannot be repeated too often) that all awaits His coming.

This is the age of His absence, but the coming age shall be characterized by His presence.[13] Not an isolated event, albeit Scripture tells us that a series of manifestations of Christ will make its course, but a new attitude toward men—immediate divine action both in blessing and in judgment. For while the covert atheism of these days of ours scoffs at the thought that the prayer which He Himself has put into our lips could ever be fulfilled, His believing people know that His kingdom is certainly coming, and that His will shall be done on earth.

These pages are a humble effort to unfold some of the many glories of our Lord Jesus Christ. To all the redeemed He is Saviour and Lord but He is also the Messiah, and King of Israel. More than this, and higher, He is the Son of Man, "King of kings and Lord of lords," "the Heir of all things," "the Firstborn of all creation." And above and beyond all this is His supreme glory as the Son of God, the glory which He had with the Father before the world was.

And there is but *one* Lord Jesus Christ. The Christ of Nazareth and Calvary is He who will consume the lawless

---

[10]See Alford's Commentary on Matthew 12:43-45.
[11]Revelation 11:15. *Basileia*, translated "kingdoms" in A.V., means dominion or sovereignty.
[12]Romans 8:21, R.V.
[13]Such is the meaning of the word *parousia*, which our English Bible renders "coming."

one by the breath of His mouth, and destroy him by the manifestation of His presence. And that same awful glory it was that overwhelmed the beloved disciple in the Patmos vision; for His eyes are as a flame of fire, and His countenance is as the sun shineth in its strength. Not even the holiest of mortal men can stand in the presence of the glory of God; but so perfect is our redemption that we are called to rejoice in hope of it. And the time is coming when "this mortal shall have put on immortality"; and then shall be fulfilled the prayer of the betrayal night, for when thus "changed" it will be our privilege and joy to behold the glory of our glorious Lord and Saviour.

APPENDICES[1]

NOTE TO CHAPTER 4 [2]

"IF THE Father begat the Son, He who was begotten had a beginning of existence. So there was a time when the Son did not exist." Thus Arius argued; and when inexorable logic deduces error from premises that are deemed true, it behooves us to test our premises again by an appeal to Scripture. And it is not a matter of opinion, but of fact, that neither in respect of His "eternal Sonship," nor even of His human birth, does Holy Scripture ever speak of the Son as "begotten of the Father."[3] And this is the more significant because the word is used so emphatically with reference to His resurrection from the dead.

But, it will be asked, is He not called "the only begotten Son of God"? This question has been already answered (see p. 40 *ante*), and it only remains to notice a most deplorable and distressing inference that is based upon the misreading of the term.

The language of theology on this subject is popularly misconstrued to mean that at the Incarnation the Deity took

---

[1]This Appendix was not ready when the proofs were submitted to the Bishop of Durham.

[2]I have written on this subject with hesitation, but under a pressing sense of the need of dealing with it.

The time is near when "the Christian miracles" will be accepted as facts, but explained on natural principles; for the crassly stupid infidelity of the past is dying out. (Dr. Harnack's reference to miracles in "What is Christianity?" points to this.) I heard of a private meeting of medical men in London last winter at which it was gravely urged that a virgin birth was possible as a natural phenomenon! The Rationalist could thus admit that the Lord was born of a virgin, without admitting that He was "conceived of the Holy Ghost."

[3]Matthew 1:20 does not conflict with this statement.

the place of a husband to the Virgin Mary. In regard to such a mystery as the Incarnation our part is to keep to the very words of Holy Scripture; and the language of Scripture is unequivocal and plain. As to His human birth, the Lord was "the Seed of the Woman." But it will be asked, how is that possible? The answer is supplied by Matthew 1:20 and Luke 1:35. The virgin birth was altogether miraculous; but if the popular belief were well founded, His birth would have been miraculous only in the sense of being unnatural.

Those who have learned to look for absolute accuracy in the language of Scripture will not fail to mark the angel's words: "Therefore that holy thing that shall be born of thee *shall be called* the Son of God." That birth did not constitute Him Son of God, yet had it not been a *virgin* birth, Mary's son could have had no possible claim to such a title.

The Rationalist trades upon the fact that the virgin birth has no place in the teaching of the Epistles. And Christians often fail to understand the omission. But the reason of it is plain. While the rejection of the virgin birth would undermine the faith, the acceptance of it (as Unitarianism abundantly proves) is incompatible with denying the Deity of Christ, and His Deity is the foundation truth of Christianity. The truth of His Sonship as implied in the virgin birth is merged in the truth that He was the Son of God in a vastly higher sense; and, as we have seen, that great truth is in the warp and woof of every part of the New Testament.

But this is not all. Unless the Gospel narratives be altogether unreliable and worthless, it is certain that Mary's firstborn was not the son of Joseph. The alternative to the virgin birth, therefore, would be that the Lord of Glory belonged to that unfortunate class which the divine law excluded from "the congregation of the Lord" (Deut. 23:2) and this being so, it is amazing that any one could expect to find an assertion of it in the doctrinal teaching of the Epistles. The whole question of the virgin birth is settled and silenced by the truth of the Lord's Deity.

The word "firstborn" claims notice here. In its ordinary use *prōtotokos* means a woman's first child, being a male. But Hebrews 12:23 gives proof that it acquired a figurative or spiritual significance, suggested by, but wholly apart from, its common meaning. For every individual in the particular company of the redeemed there designated is a "firstborn", and it is clearly used as a title of special dignity and privilege. This being so, it would be ignorant and wrong to narrow its application to our Divine Lord by reference to the virgin birth, or to construe it as implying in any way a limitation of His Deity.

The coincidence is striking that this word, like *monogenes*, occurs just nine times in Scripture. In Matthew 1:25 and Luke 2:7, it is used in its ordinary acceptation, the inference being that Mary had other children. In Hebrews 11:28 it is used by way of historic reference; and Hebrews 12:23 I have already noticed. The other passages where it occurs are Romans 8:29, Colossians 1:15, 18, Hebrews 1:6, Revelation 1:5. In the sphere of creation the term "firstborn" can be applied to the Lord only as a title of dignity and glory. And this is presumably its significance in those passages also which relate to the resurrection. If there be any reference to the ordinary meaning of the word, it is noteworthy that the "order" indicated in 1 Corinthians 15:23 is priority of rank.

"WHAT does he mean?" some may ask in laying down the tenth chapter of this book. To explain my meaning, therefore, I take up at random four documents now before me.

The first is a syllabus of services in a certain West End church which is noted for a true ministry. And among the subjects of addresses announced, I here find "The Parables of Jesus," and "Scenes in the Life of Jesus." Lectures were once announced under these same headings in a notorious "Hall of Science" in London. The profane infidel and the devout Christian thus agree in naming the Lord Jesus Christ in the same free and easy fashion.

The next is a theological work by a Professor in one of the principal Theological Colleges in America. The author is a devout and enlightened student of Scripture, and his book is of great merit and real value. The present volume, indeed, has benefited by help derived from it. But the manner in which it habitually uses "the simple name" might suggest that some infidel had got hold of the MS. and had struck out every title of reverence. It is "Jesus" everywhere. Only twenty times is the Lord named as "Jesus" in all the Epistles of the New Testament, and yet He is so named twenty-two times in the two concluding paragraphs of the last chapter of this book.

The third is a publisher's circular about a work entitled "Jesus according to St. Mark," by a clergyman who is a Fellow of an Oxford College, and Examining Chaplain to a Bishop. "It endeavors to answer the question, What kind of a person did St. Mark, or his informant, St. Peter, think Jesus to be? Under the heads of 'Jesus' family and friends,' 'Jesus' way of life,' 'Jesus' mind,' 'Jesus' social outlook,' 'Jesus' morality,' and 'Jesus' religion,' it approaches the final subject of 'Jesus Himself.' " Had the book been written by Tom Paine or Voltaire, the title and headings would have been the same, save that the "Saint" before the name of the Evangelist would probably have been omitted. "Jesus" always; but *Saint* Mark! Is it not plain that the "Jesus" of this deplorable book is the dead Buddha of the Rationalist? Could any one to whom our Lord Jesus Christ is a living person—"our great God and Saviour," before whose judgment-seat we all shall stand—write of Him, or even think of Him, after this fashion?

The last document in my list is a "book of piety" by an American writer who seems to be a *persona grata* on advanced evangelical platforms on both sides of the Atlantic. It is a deplorable book, the evil influence of which is all the greater because it is so subtle. It is fitted to promote a "Christ after the flesh" religion of a kind that charms the mere religionist, and deceives and corrupts even spiritual Christians—a religion which puts sentiment in place of faith, and the expression of that sentiment in the place of the divine revelation of the Lord Jesus Christ.[1]

Though a book of this kind enjoys a fleeting popularity because it panders to the desire of the natural man to bring "Jesus" down to his own level, it is happily short-lived. But it is otherwise with works such as find a place on the shelves of every theological library. And most of our recent theological literature is so definitely "run in a rationalistic mould," that it is unwholesome reading for Christians. And this is true even of books written by men who pose as champions of orthodoxy. Here, *e.g.*, is a typical sentence from the pen of one such: "Jesus was a very complex character." Can a man who writes thus have any real knowledge of the Lord before whom he has to stand in judgment?

---

[1] I am happy in the conviction that if I were in my grave, not even my own wife would write about me for publication after the fashion of this writer's "Talks about Jesus."

The historian who has true historical genius studies the records of the past in order to put himself back, as it were, into the life of the people of whom he writes, that he may be able to think as they thought and feel as they felt. And if we study the New Testament in this spirit, we shall realize in some measure the amazement and distress which any one of the early disciples would feel, if he returned to earth today, at finding that Christians constantly name the Lord of Glory after the example of the vagabond Jewish exorcists of the Acts. In his day, he would tell us, people declared themselves at once as unbelievers or disciples by the way in which they spoke of Him.

As proof that there can be nothing unseemly in speaking of the Lord as "Jesus," or "Jesus Christ,"[2] it is often urged that many reverent and spiritual men habitually name Him thus. But were it not for this there would be no need to write upon the subject at all. And surely the question for us is not as to the habits and practices of Christian men, but as to the teaching of Scripture and the expressed will of the Lord Himself.

If the question is to be settled by the practice of Christians, it was settled in the days of the Fathers. Though here we should distinguish between "the Apostolic Fathers" and their successors. For writings such as Clement's "Epistle to the Corinthians" and Polycarp's "Epistle to the Philippians" definitely follow the New Testament tradition in the way they name the Lord; whereas later Patristic writings give proof that, in this as in other respects, the leaven was already working which (as Froude aptly expresses it somewhere) changed the religion of Christ into the Christian religion.

---

[2] In the days when I frequented club smoking-rooms I used to hear Him called "J.C." And I believe, strange to say, that so far from this being intentionally profane, it was due to a perverted sense of reverence which shunned the use of the sacred name.

In the Gospels, as already noticed, the Lord is named narratively as "Jesus" some 600 times, but never once in the Epistles. Eight times in Hebrews, and in eight passages in the Epistles of Paul, He is called by His personal name; and in every instance its occurrence indicates some doctrinal significance or special emphasis. The following is the list of the passages in question. I will preface it merely by repeating that His disciples never spoke of Him to one another save as Master or Lord:

Romans 3:26.—This is dealt with in Chapter X.

Romans 8:11.—Here the emphatic reference to the humiliation appears plainly from the words which immediately follow.

II Corinthians 4:5.—"Your servants for Jesus' sake." This is perhaps the only passage in the Epistles that presents a difficulty. And such being the case, surely it ought to be explained on the same principle. It is certainly not for the sake of euphony or rhythm that in the same sentence the Apostle calls Him "Jesus" and "Christ Jesus the Lord."

II Corinthians 4:10-14.—Here the emphatic contrast between "Jesus" and "the Lord Jesus" is evident. "The life of Jesus" is the life He lived on earth; the life of Christ would be the vital principle which He shares with His redeemed people.

Ephesians 4:21.—This is dealt with in Chapter X.

Philippians 2:10.—This is dealt with in Chapter X.

I Thessalonians 1:10.—He is named three times in the preceding verses as the Lord Jesus Christ; here, as Jesus, God's Son, from heaven. It is not really a case in point. (Cf. I John 1:7.)

I Thessalonians 4:14.—The emphasis on the personal name is clear, and an intelligent exegesis of the passage will bring out its doctrinal significance. An *excursus* upon the subject here would be an undue digression, and the writer must take the liberty of referring to his book "The Way," p. 118 and App. II. Our versions here give exposition, not translation. The Greek reads, "If we believe that Jesus died and rose again, even so them also who were put to sleep through Jesus will God bring with Him." Which means that the Lord was the cause of their death; *i.e.* they were martyred because they were Christians. The words are not a doctrinal statement about the holy dead—that is the scope of verse 16—but a message of comfort expressly *from the Lord Himself* (verse 15) about those for whom the Thessalonians were mourning. The popular phrase, "sleeping in Jesus" is not scriptural.

The words "another Jesus" in II Corinthians 11:4 have obviously no bearing on the present question. Neither have the words of I Corinthians 12:4 as they appear in the original. "Anathema Jesus" was presumably used by profane Jews; and the Apostle contrasts it with "Lord Jesus"—the mode in which the disciples addressed Him and spoke of Him.

The Revisers' reading of Galatians 6:17 exemplifies the importance of accuracy in the use of the Lord's names. Their devotion to the three oldest MSS.—the layman's usual blunder in giving undue weight to "direct" evidence—has here led to a deplorable perversion of the Apostle's words.

"The *stigmata* of Jesus" must be explained (according to the well-known incident in the life of St. Francis of Assisi) as the wound-prints which "the Man of Sorrows" bore in His body. But however they may be interpreted, it seems incredible that such words could have been penned by the Apostle Paul. The meaning of his actual words—"the *stigmata* of the Lord Jesus"—is not doubtful. It was a practice with slave-owners to brand their slaves, and the scars of his sufferings for Christ's sake were to him the brand-marks by which his Divine Master claimed him to be His devoted slave.

The passages in Hebrews are 2:9, 4:14, 6:20, 7:22, 10:19, 12:2 and 24, and 13:12. (The R.V. adds 3:1.)

Hebrews 4:14 may be eliminated, for, as we have seen, "Jesus, the Son of God," was to the Israelite a title of the highest solemnity, connoting absolute Deity. And in 2:9, 6:20, 12:2, and 13:12, the reference to the Lord's humiliation and "witness unto death" is unmistakable. Hebrews 6:20 ("the forerunner") may be bracketed with 12:2; and 7:22 with 4:14.

These are the only passages in the Epistles of the New Testament in which the Lord is mentioned by His personal name. To use them as an excuse for the prevailing practice of naming Him with unholy familiarity is to bring Scripture into contempt, for a gulf separates even our most solemn utterances from the inspired language of Holy Scripture.

It is noteworthy that while "the simple name" is never used narratively in the Epistles, it is so used in the first chapter of Acts (verses 1, 14, and 16), which is in a sense the conclusion of the Third Gospel. And two or three other passages may seem to be in the same category, though perhaps they ought to be otherwise explained. It is also remarkable that in Acts 1:11, as in Revelation 14:12 and 19:10, the Lord is thus designated by angels. And the Lord Himself used the name of His humiliation in arresting Saul of Tarsus (Acts 9:5), as He does again in Revelation 22:16. What has been said of the use of the name "Jesus" in the Epistles applies with special force to the Apostolic preaching recorded in Acts; as, e.g., in 2:32 and 36. And still greater emphasis attaches to "Jesus of Nazareth," as a name not only of humiliation, but of reproach (see footnote 7 in Chapter X).

With reference to the few occurrences of "Jesus Christ" in Acts, the remarks offered in Chapter X apply with full force. The Lord is never thus named to *Gentiles* (for the R.V. omits 8:37).

I would here repeat the words quoted on a preceding page, that "the modern familiarity of use of the simple name *Jesus* has little authority in Apostolic usage." But in view of the foregoing analysis of Scripture, I would go further, and maintain that, to *familiarity* of use, the New Testament lends no sanction whatever. It is generally due to ignorance, indifference, or sheer carelessness. To call Him "Jesus" saves time and breath. Moreover, it is popular with hearers and readers—a Christ-after-the-flesh cult is always popular—and if *we* like it, what does it matter? He is of no account whatever!

To call a fellow-man by his personal name betokens great familiarity; and if there be Christians who have gained such a position with their Lord and Saviour, it is not for us to judge them. But we who claim no such place must not allow ourselves to be betrayed by their example into thoughts or modes of speech which His presence would rebuke and silence. If we really desire "to sanctify Christ in our hearts as Lord," we shall be careful and eager to own Him as Lord with our lips. And all influences that hinder the realization of that desire are unwholesome, and we do well to shun them.

"Ye do show the Lord's death till he come" (I Cor. 11:26). In these words we have the faith and hope of Christianity; and no one who lets go any part of the truth they express has any right to the name of Christian. For to reject the hope of the Coming is as really a mark of apostasy as to deny the Atonement. And no spiritual Christian will need to be reminded of the significance of the word, the *Lord's* death. "The death of Jesus" might mean merely the end of His earthly life in Judea long ago. This indeed is the ruling thought in the religion of Christendom, the crucifix being the symbol of it. But it is not through the slough of nineteen centuries of apostasy that we reach the Cross. Faith brings us into the presence of the Lord in His glory, and we rest upon His words—"I am he that liveth and was dead, and behold, I am alive for evermore" (Rev. 1:18). "We know that the Son of God is come"—that is the Christian's past. "He is now at the right hand of God . . . for us"—that is his present. And as for the future, "We are looking for the Saviour, the Lord Jesus Christ" (I John 5:20; Rom. 8:34; Phil. 3:20).

Our hymn-books contain many a hymn which Christians would discard or alter if they knew what it meant "to sanctify

Christ in their hearts *as Lord."* I take, for instance, the hymn beginning—

> "Sweet Saviour, bless us ere we go,"

with the refrain at the end of every verse—

> "O gentle Jesu, be our light."

Who is the Being whom people are taught to address in such terms and in such a manner? One moment's intelligent thought will satisfy any one that he is not our risen and glorified Lord and Saviour. His personal name occurs many hundreds of times in the New Testament, but *never once with an adjective.* Not even in the days of His humiliation did His chosen disciples ever address Him thus. The plain truth is that this "sweet, gentle Jesu" is a mere idol. The same tendency in human nature which leads some to worship a mythical Virgin Mary, declares itself in impersonating this mythical Jesus, who is an object of sentiment, and not of faith. And this tendency is so deep and general that in scores of hymns we find this utterly unchristian, "O Jesus," when the rhythm of the verse is marred by it, and would be saved by the use of the Christian mode of address, "Lord Jesus."

"Ye call Me Master and Lord, and ye say well." These are His own words; and surely this is enough for the true disciple!

A friend of mine tells of the death-bed words of a revered Christian minister by whom he himself was brought to the Lord. In response to the inquiry, "Safe in the arms of Jesus?" the old saint opened his eyes, and replied with a smile, "No, no; *at His feet."* It was the attitude of the beloved disciple in the Patmos vision. We should never allow a hymn-book to betray us into using words which we would not use if the Lord were present, or if we really believed that He was listening.

Safe in Jehovah's keeping,
　Led by His glorious arm,
God is Himself my refuge,
　A present help from harm.
Fears may at times distress me,
　Griefs may my soul annoy;
God is my strength and portion,
　God my exceeding joy.

Safe in Jehovah's keeping,
　Safe in temptation's hour,
Safe in the midst of perils,
　Kept by Almighty power.
Safe when the tempest rages,
　Safe though the night be long;
E'en when my sky is darkest
　God is my strength and song.

Sure is Jehovah's promise,
　Nought can my hope assail;
Here is my soul's sure anchor,
　Entered within the veil.
Blest in His love eternal,
　What can I want beside!
Safe through the blood that cleanseth,
　Safe in the Christ that died.

SIR ROBERT ANDERSON
LIBRARY SERIES

THE COMING PRINCE
This is the standard work on the marvelous prophecy of Daniel about the AntiChrist and the Seventy Weeks. It deals fully with the details of the chronology and with the vexing questions of the last of the Seventy Sevens.

FORGOTTEN TRUTHS
The author shares valuable insight into the difficulty for some people caused by the delay of our Lord's return, as well as other truths seemingly irreconcilable because of finite human minds.

THE GOSPEL AND ITS MINISTRY
A study of such basic Christian truths as Grace, Reconcilation, Justification and Sanctification. In the author's own direct, yet devotional, style these truths are stated, then emphasized; so that the skeptic becomes convinced and the believer is blessed.

THE LORD FROM HEAVEN
A devotional treatment of the doctrine of the Deity of Christ. This differs from other works in that it offers indirect testimony of the Scriptures as to the validity of this doctrine. This book is not written to settle doctrinal controversy, but rather it is a Bible study that will deepen the student's conviction, while giving a warm devotional approach.

Sir Robert Anderson Library

REDEMPTION TRUTHS
The author presents unique insights on the gift offer of salvation, the glory of Sonship and the grandeur of eternity's splendor.

THE SILENCE OF GOD
If God really cares, why has He let millions on earth suffer, starve and fall prey to the ravages of nature? Why has He been silent for nearly two millennia? The author gives a thorough and Scriptural answer. He also discusses the subject of miracles today with excellent answers. Here is a "must" for serious Bible students.

TYPES IN HEBREWS
A study of the types found in the book of Hebrews. Anderson ties the revelation of God to the Hebrew nation to the full revelation of the Church of Jesus Christ, with the premise that God's provision for the Jew was a forerunner of the blessings for the Christian. The author moves from type to type with his own pithy comments and then augments them with the comments of his nineteenth century contemporaries.